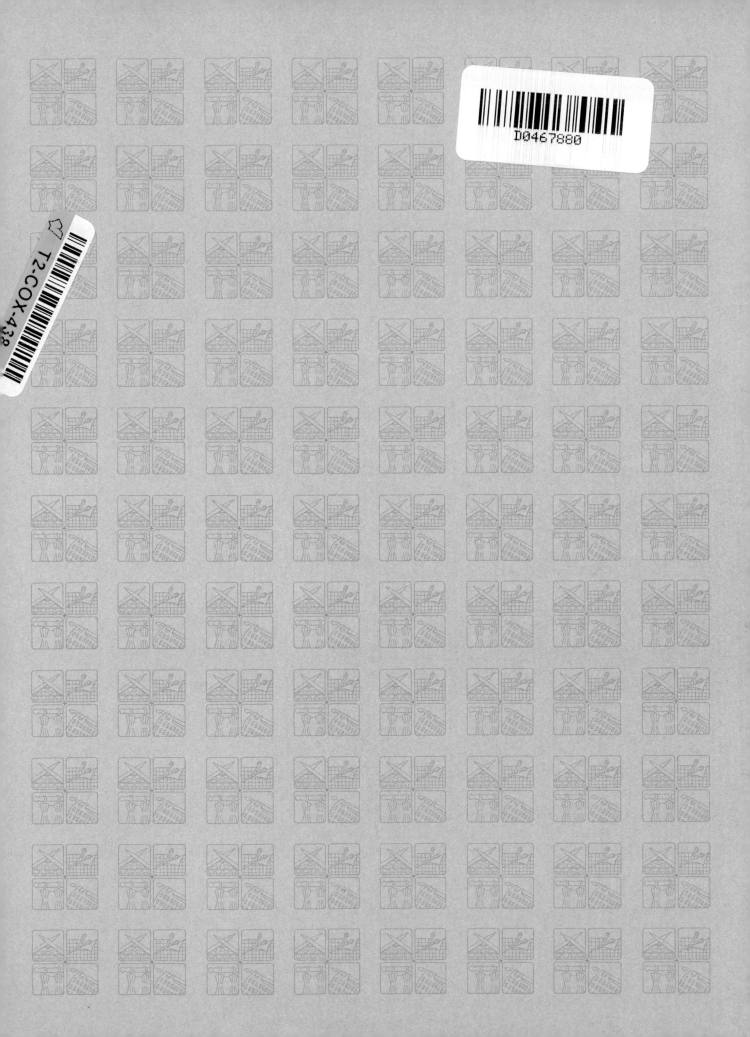

Stitch by Stitch

Volume 15

TORSTAR BOOKS

NEW YORK · TORONTO

Stitch by Stitch

TORSTAR BOOKS INC.
41 MADISON AVENUE
SUITE 2900
NEW YORK, NY 10010

Knitting and crochet abbreviations

approx = approximately	in = inch(es)	sl st = slip stitch
beg = begin(ning)	inc = increas(e)(ing)	sp = space(s)
ch = chain(s)	K = knit	st(s) = stitch(es)
cm = centimeter(s)	oz = ounce(s)	tbl = through back of
cont = continue(ing)	P = purl	loop(s)
dc = double crochet	patt = pattern	tog = together
dec = decreas(e)(ing)	psso = pass slipped	tr = triple crochet
dtr = double triple	stitch over	WS = wrong side
foll = follow(ing)	rem = remain(ing)	wyib = with yarn in
g = gram(s)	rep = repeat	back
grp = group(s)	RS = right side	wyif = with yarn in front
hdc = half double	sc = single crochet	yd = yard(s)
crochet	sl = slip	yo = yarn over

A guide to the pattern sizes

		10	12	14	16	18	20
Bust	in	32½	34	36	38	40	42
	cm	83	87	92	97	102	107
Waist	in	25	26½	28	30	32	34
	cm	64	67	71	76	81	87
Hips	in	34½	36	38	40	42	44
	cm	88	92	97	102	107	112

Torstar Books also offers a range of acrylic book stands, designed to keep instructional books such as *Stitch by Stitch* open, flat and upright while leaving the hands free for practical work.

For information write to Torstar Books Inc., 41 Madison Avenue, Suite 2900, New York, NY 10010.

Library of Congress Cataloging in Publication Data
Main entry under title:

Stitch by stitch.

Includes index.
1. Needlework. I. Torstar Books (Firm)
TT705.S74 1984   746.4   84-111
ISBN 0-920269-00-1 (set)

9876543

© Marshall Cavendish Limited 1985

Printed in Belgium

ISBN 0–920269–15–X (Volume 15)

Step-by-Step Crochet Course

66 Shaping in Tunisian crochet
    Increasing one stitch
    Decreasing one stitch
    Increasing several stitches
    Decreasing several stitches
    Pattern for a girl's dress and pinafore

67 Twisted and crossed stitches in
        Tunisian crochet
    Stitch Wise: more twisted and crossed
        stitch patterns
    Pattern for a woman's long jacket

68 Buttonholes
    Bobbles
    Stitch Wise: more simple Tunisian
        stitches
    Patterns for two cardigans for
        a baby

69 Crochet on canvas
    Working chains on canvas
    Crochet squares worked on canvas
    Ways of joining canvas
    Two patterns for crochet canvas bags

Step-by-Step Knitting Course

66 Working a neckline with lapels
    Working a separate collar with lapels
    Pattern for a boy's jacket

67 Introduction to patchwork knitting
    Working patches in strips
    Designing patchwork with squares and
        triangles
    Patterns for a patchwork baby blanket
        and child's sweater

68 Making a fabric with irregular
        patchwork shapes
    Pattern for a crazy patchwork coat

69 Working patchwork texture in
        separate pieces
    Working patchwork texture within
        a fabric
    Pattern for a patchwork sweater

Contents

70 Knitting in rounds to make gloves 55
Stitch Wise: Italian and French
patterns
Patterns for man's and woman's
hat, scarf and glove sets 58

Step-by-Step Sewing Course

64 Quilting 60
Hand quilting
Frog fastenings
Chinese ball buttons
Pattern for a quilted jacket:
adapting the pattern 63
directions for making 65

65 Working with skins and leather-like
fabrics 68
Cut-work motifs on non-fraying fabrics
Pattern for a vest and skirt:
adapting the patterns 70
directions for making 72

66 False fly fastening 77
Pattern for a hooded raincoat with
detachable lining (1):
adapting the pattern 78

67 Detachable hood 82
Detachable lining
Pattern for a hooded raincoat (2):
directions for making 83

Step-by-Step Needlework Course

18 Machine embroidery – special effects 89
Satin stitch effects
Transferring a design – perforation
method
A machine-embroidered panel 90

Extra Special Crochet

Strawberry motif sweater 92
Baby's blanket and sleeping bag 95

Extra Special Knitting

Beaded sweater 98
Slipper socks 100

Extra Special Sewing

Dress with knitted inserts 102
Hat with knitted bands 106

Needlework Extra

Needlepoint pineapple picture 109

Homemaker

Fold-away mattress 112
Quilted lining and cushion for a blanket
box 116
Kitchen chair cushions 120
Topsy-turvy doll 123

Shoestring

Heart-shaped pincushions 40
Wooly dolls 54
Vinyl shopping bag 76

Crochet / COURSE 66

*Shaping in Tunisian crochet
*Increasing one stitch
*Decreasing one stitch
*Increasing several stitches
*Decreasing several stitches
*Pattern for a girl's dress and pinafore

Shaping in Tunisian crochet

Tunisian crochet can be shaped by increasing or decreasing the number of loops made in a row. In this way armholes, sleeves, necks, etc., are shaped to make fitted garments. This course gives instructions for single and multiple increases and decreases. It is followed by a pattern for a simple shaped dress and pinafore.

When working fitted garments you will have to test your gauge accurately. This is done in the same way as for ordinary crochet by making a sample piece at least 4in (10cm) square and then measuring the number of stitches and rows per in (cm). If you are a beginner, make sure that you can work Tunisian crochet with a relatively even tension before beginning any garments. To test this, make two sample pieces and check the consistency of your gauge.

It is often necessary when shaping garments to add several stitches at once at the edge of the fabric. In Tunisian

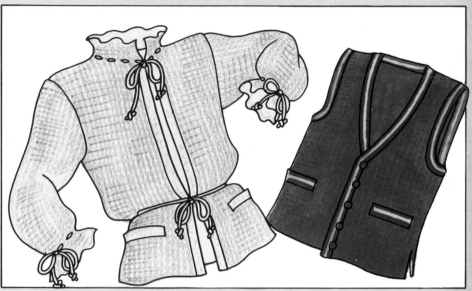

crochet this is done by working new loops onto a base of chain stitches in the same way as when working the base row. Several stitches must be decreased at the edge when shaping armholes or shoulders on a fitted garment.

Increasing one stitch

There are several ways to increase single stitches in Tunisian crochet. The method given here produces a neat, tight increase which will not leave holes in the fabric. It therefore gives the best results when shaping garments where the increase needs to be as invisible as possible. You can increase using this method with most Tunisian crochet stitch patterns. When working a single increase in the middle of a row, use the same method given for increasing at the side edge of the work. In this case your pattern will tell you where the increased stitches should be placed.

1 An increase at the right-hand edge is worked at the beginning of a loop row. Insert the hook **into** the horizontal chain stitch, made by the last return row, between the first and second vertical loops below.

2 Wind the yarn over the hook and draw a loop through the chain stitch.

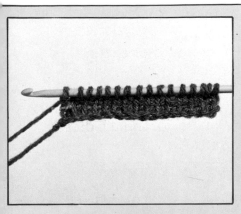

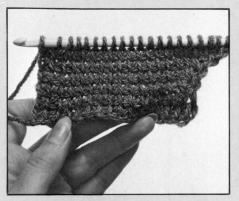

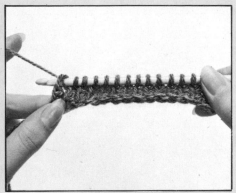

3 Then complete the loop row in the usual way by drawing a loop through each vertical strand in the row below.

4 Work the return row in the normal way, incorporating the extra loop made at the beginning of the previous row into the pattern. This sample shows single stitches increased in every loop row on the right-hand edge.

5 An increase on the left-hand edge is worked at the end of a loop row. Before making the last loop insert the hook **into** the horizontal chain between the last two vertical loops in the row below.

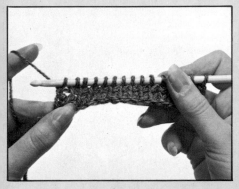

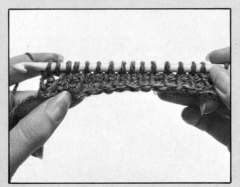

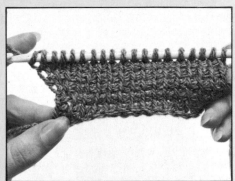

6 Wind the yarn over the hook and draw a loop through the chain stitch.

7 Draw a loop through the last vertical loop as shown here. Work the return row in the usual way, incorporating the extra loop into the pattern.

8 This sample shows single stitches increased on every loop row on the left-hand edge.

Decreasing one stitch

Like increasing, decreasing single stitches in Tunisian crochet is worked in the loop row. The method given here for decreasing at the right- and left-hand edges can also be used in the middle of a row. Some patterns may call for several single decreases to be placed across a row, in which case the decreases should be spaced at regular intervals. The pattern will usually stipulate the exact placement. If you want to decrease in the exact center of a row, you should use "paired decreases." This means working two stitches together before the center stitch and two stitches after the center stitch. Paired central decreases should only be worked on alternate rows, rather than on every row.

1 For a decrease at the right-hand edge begin the loop row by inserting the hook from right to left behind the second and third vertical loops in the row below in the same way as when working one stitch.

2 Wind the yarn over the hook and draw a loop through both strands, thus decreasing one stitch.

Fred Mancini

continued

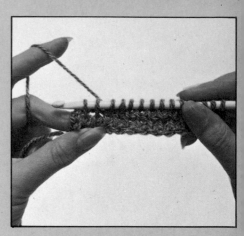

3 Then continue the loop row in the usual way, making loops into each vertical strand in the row below.

4 This sample shows single decreases worked in every row at the right-hand edge.

5 For a decrease at the left-hand edge, work all the loops in a loop row except the last three stitches. Insert the hook into the next two vertical loops below.

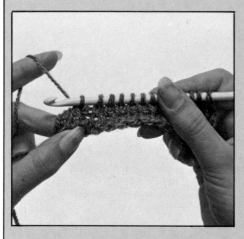

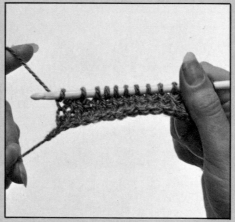

6 Wind the yarn over the hook and draw a loop through both strands to decrease one stitch.

7 Now insert hook into last vertical strand and draw a loop through as shown. Work return row in usual way.

8 This sample shows one stitch decreased on every loop row at the left-hand edge.

Increasing several stitches

1 For the right-hand edge, at the end of a return row work as many chains as the number of stitches you want to add. Insert the hook into the second chain from the hook. Wind the yarn over the hook and draw a loop through.

2 Make loops into each added chain and then into each vertical loop in the row below including the edge stitch.

3 On the next return row work all the new loops off the hook in the same way as the original loops. Any number of stitches can be added to the edge in this way.

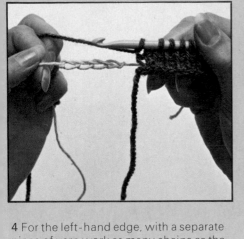

4 For the left-hand edge, with a separate piece of yarn work as many chains as the number of stitches you want to add and hold in left hand ready to start working.

5 At the end of a loop row insert the hook into the first chain. Wind the yarn over the hook and draw a loop through.

6 Make loops into each of the chain stitches. Then work the return row in the usual way. The added piece of chain is shown in a different color to indicate that it has been made with a separate length of yarn, but would normally be worked in same color yarn.

Decreasing several stitches

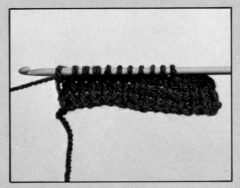

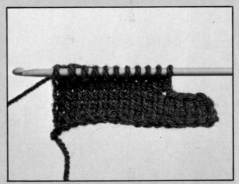

1 For the right-hand edge, at the beginning of a loop row insert the hook into the second vertical loop in the row below. Wind the yarn over the hook and draw a loop through the vertical strand and the loop on the hook.

2 Work over each stitch to be decreased in the same way, drawing the yarn through both the vertical strand and the loop on the hook. Then begin the loop row and make loops across the rest of the row.

3 Any number of stitches can be decreased with this method. Although it can be used for single decreases it will not produce as smooth an edge as is made by working two loops together.

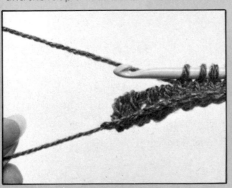

4 For the left-hand edge, work across a loop row until there are as many stitches left as the number to be decreased.

5 Begin the return row by drawing through first one loop and then two loops at a time to the end of the row.

6 If you find that this decreased edge is not firm enough take a separate length of yarn and work slip stitch over it as you would on a right-side multiple decrease.

Fred Mancini

7

Girl's dress and pinafore

Tunisian crochet need not mean thick, heavy fabric and here's proof: a pretty dress and a pinafore with French knots.

Sizes
Dress To fit 20[22:24]in (51[56:61]cm). Length, 18¼[18¾:19¾]in (46[48:50]cm). Sleeve, 8[8¾:9½]in (20[22:24]cm).
Apron Length from center front neck 13½[13½:14¾]in (34[34:38]cm).
Note: Directions for larger sizes are in brackets []; if there is only one set of figures it applies to all sizes.

Materials
- 8[8:10]oz (200[200:250]g) of a lightweight mercerized cotton in main color (A)
- 4oz (100g) in contrasting color (B)
- Size G (4.50mm) Tunisian crochet hook
- Size E (3.50mm) crochet hook
- 4 buttons for dress; 1 for pinafore

Gauge
25 sts and 52 rows (26 vertical loops) to 4in (10cm) with size G (4.50mm) hook.

Dress

Back
*Using size G (4.50mm) Tunisian hook and A, make 96[102:110]ch. Work in plain Tunisian stitch (see Volume 14, page 21) for 24 rows (12 vertical loops).
25th row Dec one loop (see page 5), work 26[28:30] sts, dec one loop, work 34[36:40] sts, dec one loop, work 26[28:30] sts, dec one loop, work 1.
26th row Work back.
Work 22 rows (11 vertical loops).
Next row Dec one loop, work 25[27:29] sts, dec one loop, work 32[34:38] sts, dec one loop, work 25[27:29] sts, dec one loop, work 1.
Next row Work back.
Work 22 rows. Cont to dec in this way on next and every foll 23rd row until 72[78:86] loops rem. Cont straight until work measures 13½[13¾:14¼]in (34[35:36]cm).
Shape armholes
Next 2 rows Sl st across first 4 loops, work to within last 4 loops, then work back.
Dec one loop at each end of next and every other row until 54[60:66] loops rem.*
Next row Work back.*
Divide for neck
Next 2 rows Work 31[34:37] loops, then work back.
Cont on these loops until armhole measures 4¾[5:5½]in (12[13:14]cm); end at armhole edge.
Shape shoulder
Next 2 rows Work 1 sc into each of first 6[7:8] loops, work to end, then work

back.
Rep last 2 rows twice more. Fasten off. With RS facing join A to center loop (so working 4 loops in front of first 4 corresponding loops at center) then work 27[30:33] loops. Work 2nd side to match first, reversing shaping. Using size E (3.50mm) crochet hook and A work 2 rows sc along lower edge. Fasten off.

Front
Work as back from * to *. Cont straight until armhole measures 3¼[3½:4]in (8[9:10]cm).
Shape neck
Next 2 rows Work 20[23:26] loops, then work back.
Next 2 rows Work 17[20:23] loops, dec one loop, work 1, then work back.
Next 2 rows Work 16[19:22] loops, dec one loop, work 1, then work back.
Cont on these loops until armhole measures 4¾[5:5½]in (12[13:14]cm); at armhole edge.
Shape shoulder
Next 2 rows Work 1 sc into each of first 6[7:8] loops, work to end, then work back.
Rep last 2 rows twice more. Fasten off. Skip center 14 loops, join A to next loop and work to end of row. Complete to match first side reversing shaping. Using size E (3.50mm) crochet hook and A, work 2 rows sc along lower edge. Fasten off.

Sleeves
Using size G (4.50mm) Tunisian hook and A, make 30[32:36] ch. Cont in plain Tunisian stitch inc one loop (see page 4) at each end of 25th row and every foll 24th row (i.e. every 12th vertical loop row) until there are 38[40:44] loops. Cont straight until work measures 8[8¾:9½]in (20[22:24]cm).
Shape top
Next 2 rows Sl st across first 4 loops, work to within last 4 loops, then work back. Dec one loop at each end of next and every other row until 18[20:24] sts rem.
Next 2 rows Sl st across first 2 loops, work to within last 2 loops, then work back.
Rep last 2 rows 3 times more. Fasten off. Using size E (3.50mm) crochet hook and A, work 2 rows sc along lower edge. Fasten off.

Neck edging
Join shoulder seams. Join A to left back neck opening and using size E (3.50mm) crochet hook work 7 rows sc around

neck. Do not turn on last row but work a row of sc evenly along right back opening, turn.
Next row 1 sc into each of first 4 sc, (1 ch, skip next sc, 1 sc into each of next 7 sc) 3 times, 1 ch, skip next sc, work to end. Fasten off.

To finish
Set in sleeves, then join side and sleeve seams. Sew on buttons.

Pinafore

Using size G (4.50mm) Tunisian hook and B, make 62 ch. Cut off yarn.
Shape lower edge
Working in Tunisian stockinette st (see Volume 14, page 28) join B to 18th ch, work 26 loops, then work back.
Next 2 rows Remove hook from loop, insert hook into 14th ch, work into each of next 4 ch, work to end, then work 4 extra loops—4 loops inc at each end of row—, then work back.
Rep last 2 rows twice more.
Next 2 rows Remove hook from loop, insert hook into first ch, work into each of next 5 ch, work to end, then work into each of last 6 ch, then work back. 62 vertical loops.
Cont on these loops for 24[24:40] more rows (12[12:20] vertical loops).
Now dec one loop at each end of next and every foll 18th row until 44 loops rem.

Shape neck

Next 2 rows Work 16 loops, work back. Dec one loop at neck edge on next and every other row until 10 loops rem. Cont on these loops for strap, until strap fits around to center back neck.

Next 2 rows Work 4 loops (yo) twice for buttonhole, skip next 2 loops, work 4 loops, then work back. Dec one loop at each end of next and every other row until 2 loops rem. Fasten off. Skip center 14 loops then work 2nd side to match, omitting buttonhole and top shaping. Using size E (3.50mm) crochet hook and B, work 1 row sc around outer edge.

Next round *Skip next sc, work 3 dc into next sc, skip next sc, sl st into next sc,* rep from * to * all around. Fasten off.

Ties (make 2)

Using size G (4.50mm) Tunisian hook and B, make 8 ch. Work in Tunisian stockinette st for 20in (52cm). Dec one loop at each end of next and every other row until 1 loop rem. Fasten off. Work a row of sc around outer edge.

To finish

Sew ties at waist level. Sew on button. With A work rows of French knots on pinafore as shown in picture.

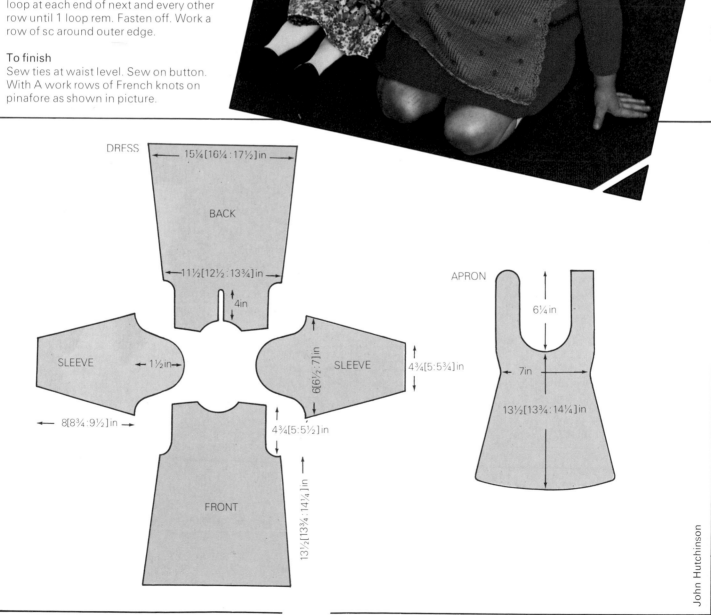

DRESS

15¼[16¼:17½]in

BACK

11½[12½:13¾]in

4in

SLEEVE   1½in

SLEEVE   4¾[5:5¾]in

6[6½:7]in

8[8¾:9½]in

4¾[5:5½]in

FRONT

13½[13¾:14¼]in

APRON

6¼in

7in

13½[13¾:14¼]in

John Hutchinson

* Twisted and crossed
  stitches in Tunisian crochet
* Stitch Wise: More twisted
  and crossed stitch patterns
* Pattern for a woman's
  long jacket

Twisted and crossed stitches in Tunisian crochet

The Victorian name for plain Tunisian stitch—fool's or idiot stitch—may not be far wrong if you consider the ease with which the technique can be mastered. But it is misleading in describing the potential of the stitch. Plain stitch is, after all, the foundation on which all of the numerous Tunisian crochet stitch patterns are based. By manipulating the vertical loops of plain stitch in various ways, you can give the fabric surface many different attractive textures. Step-by-step instructions for working twisted and crossed Tunisian stitches are given in this course.

Once you have learned crossed stitch, try combining it in stripes with plain stitches. This pattern is very attractive worked in two pale colors: one used for two loop rows of plain stitch and one for three loop rows of crossed stitch.

Twisted stitch

In plain Tunisian crochet, the vertical strands visible on the front of the fabric slant slightly to the left. For some stitch patterns, it is necessary to produce a vertical strand which slants to the right. This is done by inserting the hook from left to right, thereby twisting the loop.

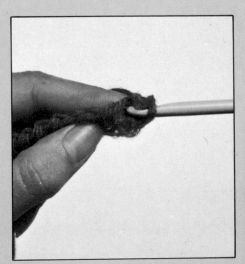

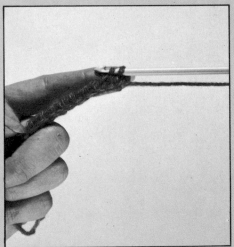

1 Make a length of chains and work the first two rows as for plain Tunisian crochet. Then on the third row insert the hook from the left to the right through the second vertical loop below. The trick in doing this is to get hold of the strand with the lip of the hook.

2 Push the tip of the hook through from left to right upward. If you have passed the hook through the loop correctly, the long vertical strand from the front of the work should go behind the hook to the right of the short vertical strand from the back of the work.

continued

Fred Mancini

11

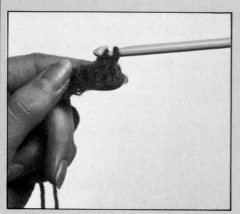

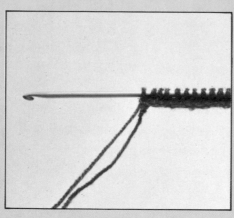

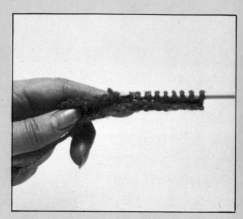

3 Wind the yarn over the hook and draw a loop through.

4 Continue working across the row from right to left, picking up loops as in steps 2 and 3.

5 Work a return row as for plain stitch, drawing the yarn through the first loop on the hook and then through two loops at a time to the end of the row.

6 If several rows of twisted stitch are worked in succession a bias fabric is created. For this reason twisted stitch is rarely worked on its own.

7 One way to form a fabric using twisted stitch is to work it in conjunction with plain stitch. This can be done by working first a row of twisted stitch and then a row of plain stitch as shown here.

8 Here plain and twisted stitches have been worked alternately across the row to form a ribbed effect. Detailed instructions are included in the jacket directions on page 14.

Crossed stitches

Another technique used in forming Tunisian crochet stitch patterns is crossing the vertical loops over one another. When attempting this stitch, do not work it too tightly; the vertical loops need to have enough "give" to be pulled across each other easily. An attractive variation of the crossed stitch pattern right is described in Stitch Wise on page 14.

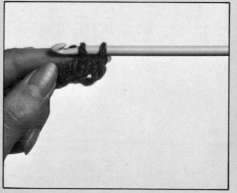

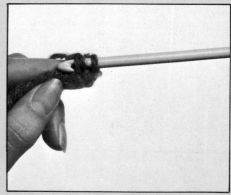

1 Make an even number of chains and work the first two rows as for plain Tunisian stitch. On the third row insert the hook from right to left through the *third* vertical loop in the row below. Wind yarn over hook and draw a loop through.

2 Now insert the hook into the second vertical loop.

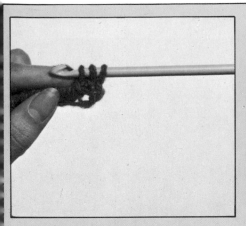

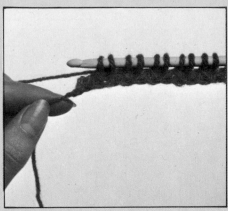

3 Wind the yarn over the hook and draw a loop through. This crosses the first two vertical loops in the row below.

4 Continue across the row in this way, skipping a vertical loop, then drawing a loop through the next vertical loop, then drawing a loop through skipped stitch.

5 When the last vertical loop is reached, insert the hook into this edge stitch. Wind the yarn over the hook and draw a loop through.

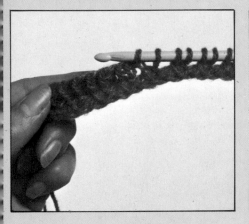

6 Work the return row as for plain stitch, drawing through first one loop on the hook then through two at a time to the end of the row.

7 Continue to work in this way to form the crossed stitch fabric.

8 When the fabric is the required length finish the top edge. After completing a return row, make one chain and insert the hook into the third vertical loop. Wind the yarn over the hook and draw a loop through.

9 Wind the yarn over the hook and draw through both loops on the hook.

10 Now insert the hook through the skipped loop and work a single crochet into it.

11 Continue across the row skipping a vertical loop and working a single crochet into the next loop, then working a single crochet into the skipped stitch. At the end of the row make a single crochet into the last loop, break the yarn and draw it through the loop on the hook.

Fred Mancini

Stitch Wise

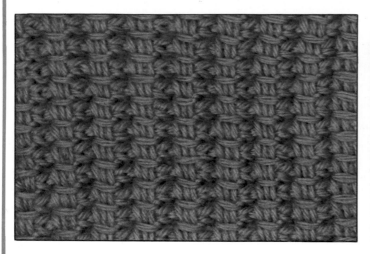

Ladder stitch

Make a multiple of 3 chains plus 2 extra.
1st row Insert hook into top loop of second ch from hook, yo and draw a loop through, *insert hook into top loop of next ch, yo and draw a loop through, rep from * to end. Do not turn.
2nd row Yo and draw through first loop on hook, *yo and draw through next 2 loops on hook, rep from * to end. Do not turn.
3rd row Skip first vertical loop, *yo from front to back, (insert hook into next vertical loop, yo and draw a loop through) 3 times, pass 4th loop from hook from right to left over last 3 loops on hook, rep from * to end, insert hook into last vertical loop, yo and draw a loop through.
4th row As 2nd.
Rows 3 and 4 form the patt and rep throughout.

Diagonal stitch

Make an even number of chains.
1st row insert hook into 2nd ch from hook, yo and draw a loop through, *insert hook into next ch, yo and draw a loop through, rep from * to end. Do not turn work.
2nd row Yo and draw through first loop on hook, *yo and draw through 2 loops on hook, rep from * until there is one loop on hook. Do not turn work.
3rd row Insert hook into 3rd vertical loop in row below, yo and draw a loop through, insert hook into 2nd vertical loop, yo and draw a loop through, *skip a vertical loop and insert hook into next vertical loop, yo and draw a loop through, insert hook into next skipped st, yo and draw a loop through, rep from * to last st, insert hook into last loop, yo, draw loop through. Do not turn.
4th row As 2nd.
5th row Insert hook into 2nd vertical loop, yo and draw a loop through, *skip a vertical loop and insert hook into next vertical loop, yo and draw a loop through, insert hook into skipped st, yo and draw a loop through, rep from * to last 2 sts (insert hook into next vertical loop, yo and draw a loop through) twice.
Do not turn work. Rows 2 to 5 form patt and are rep throughout.

Long-line jacket

Make this jacket in a rich tweedy yarn; you'll wear it all year round.

Sizes
To fit 32-34[36-38]in (83-87[92-97]cm) bust.
Length, 34½[35½]in (87[89]cm).
Sleeve seam, 19¾in (50cm) with cuff.
Note: Directions for larger size are in brackets [ ]; if there is only one set of figures it applies to all sizes.

Materials
*46[52]oz (1300[1450]g) of a knitting worsted
Size I (6.00mm) Tunisian hook
Size H (5.50mm) crochet hook*

Gauge
14 sts and 24 rows (12 vertical loops) to 4in (10cm) in patt on size I (6.00mm)
Tunisian hook.

Right back
Using size I (6.00mm) Tunisian hook make 46[50]ch.
1st row Insert hook into 2nd ch from hook, yo and draw a loop through, *insert hook into next ch, yo and draw a loop through, rep from * to end. Do not turn work. 46[50]loops.
2nd row Yo and draw through first loop on hook, *yo and draw through next 2 loops on hook, rep from * to end.
3rd row *Insert hook from right to left through next vertical loop, yo and draw a loop through, insert hook from left to right through next vertical loop and draw a loop through, rep from * to end, insert hook from right to left into end st, yo and draw a loop through. Do not turn work. 46[50]loops.
4th row As 2nd.
The 3rd and 4th rows form the patt and are rep throughout.
5th row As 3rd.
6th row As 2nd until 3 loops rem, yo and draw through 3 loops—one loop dec at right-hand edge.
7th row Insert hook from right to left through next loop, patt to end. Do not turn work. Keeping patt correct, cont to dec at right-hand edge on every 10th row until 32[36]sts rem, then cont straight until work measures 23¼in (59cm); end with a 4th row.
Shape armhole
Next row Sl st over first 2 sts, patt to end. Do not turn. 30[34]loops.
Next row As 2nd.
**Next row As 3rd.
Next row As 6th.
Next row As 7th.
Next row As 6th.

Next 2 rows As 3rd and 4th rows. ** Rep last 6 rows from ** to ** (thus dec 2 sts in every 6 rows) 9[10] times more. 10[12] sts. Fasten off.

Left back
Work first 5 rows as right half.
6th row *Yo and draw through 2 loops, rep from * to end—one loop dec at left-hand edge.
Cont as right half, reversing shaping.

Left front
Work as right back until work measures 19¾in (50cm); end with a 3rd row.
Shape front edge
Cont to shape right-hand edge and armhole to match back, at same time dec one st at left-hand edge on next and every foll 10th [8th] row 8 [10] times in all. 2 sts. Fasten off.

Right front
Work as left front, reversing shaping.

Sleeves
Using size I (6.00mm) Tunisian hook make 32 [36]ch and work first 4 rows as back, then work 4 more rows without shaping.
Next row Inc one loop (see page 4), patt to within last loop, inc one loop, patt to end. Do not turn work. Cont in patt, inc one loop at each end of every 12th row until there are 48 [52] loops, then cont straight until sleeve measures 17in (43cm); end with a 4th row. Mark each end of last row, then work 4 more rows.
Shape top
Next row As 3rd.
Next row *Yo and draw through 2 loops, rep from * until 3 loops rem, yo and

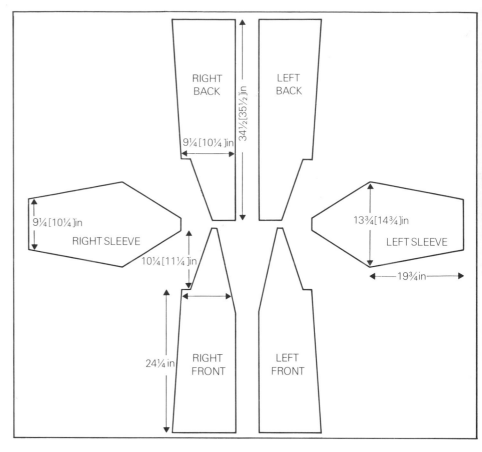

draw through 3 loops—one loop dec at each end.
Rep the 6 rows of back from ** to ** but dec at each end of row instead of one edge until 8 loops rem. Fasten off.
Cuff
With RS facing and size H (5.50mm) crochet hook work 24 [26] sc along lower edge of sleeve. Work 10 rows sc. Fasten

off.
Pockets (make 2)
Using size I (6.00mm) Tunisian hook make 20ch and work in patt for 32 rows (16 vertical loops). Change to size H (5.50mm) crochet hook. Work 4 rows sc. Fasten off.

To finish
Press or block, according to yarn used. Join center back and raglan seams, sew 4 rows above markers to bound-off sts at armholes. Join side and sleeve seams, reversing seam for cuff.
Lower border
With RS facing and size H (5.50mm) hook work 3sc into every 4 sts along lower edge. Work 4 rows sc. Fasten off.
Front border and collar
With RS facing and using size H (5.50mm) hook work 55sc along front edge to beg of shaping, 34 [39] sc to raglan, 6sc across sleeve top, 15 [17] sc across back neck, 6sc across sleeve top, 34 [39] sc along left front to beg of shaping, then 55 sc to lower edge.
Next row Work 110 [117] sc, turn.
Next row Work 15 [17] sc, turn.
Next row Work 20 [22] sc, turn.
Cont working 5 more sc on every row until the row 95 [107] sc, turn has been worked.
Next row Work in sc to end, so ending at lower edge of right front.
Next 2 rows Work in sc across all sts. Fasten off.
Press all seams. Sew on pockets.

Stefano Massimo

Crochet / COURSE 68

*Buttonholes
*Bobbles
*Stitch Wise: more simple
 Tunisian stitches
*Patterns for two cardigans
 for a baby

Buttonholes

Knitted or crocheted button and button-hole bands make attractive finishes for Tunisian crochet jackets or cardigans. However, instead of sewing on separate bands, you may prefer to work the buttonholes directly into the fabric. Either horizontal or vertical buttonholes can be worked, and instructions for both are given in this course.

Buttonholes in Tunisian crochet look better and last longer if they are strengthened and finished with buttonhole stitch. Unless you wish to highlight them, work the buttonholes in a yarn to match the main fabric.

Horizontal buttonholes

In this method the buttonhole is made by skipping stitches in a loop row and replacing these skipped stitches by winding the yarn over the hook to make a stitch. The length of the buttonhole depends on the size of the button. Allow at least $\frac{1}{2}$-$\frac{3}{4}$in (1.5-2cm) between the end of the buttonhole and the edge of the Tunisian crochet fabric.

1 Work to the position of the buttonhole on a loop row.

2 Wind the yarn once over the hook for each vertical loop being skipped in the row below.

3 Then continue making loops to the end of the loop row.

4 On the return row wind the yarn over the hook and draw through one loop on the hook. Then draw through two loops at a time, treating each yarn over hook made over the buttonhole in the same way as the other loops.

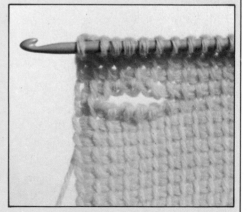

5 On the next row insert the hook from right to left under the loop made by winding yarn over hook on first buttonhole row. After making the first buttonhole, test its size by passing the button through it. If it is too small for the button to pass through easily, re-make the buttonhole and increase the number of stitches skipped. If it is too large decrease the number skipped.

Fred Mancini

17

Vertical buttonholes

These are made in much the same way as vertical buttonholes in knitting and crochet. The fabric on one side of the buttonhole is worked and then the other side is worked to the same height and the two sides are rejoined.

1 Work to the position of the buttonhole in a loop row, then work a return row, leaving the remaining stitches unworked.

2 Continue working rows until the required height is reached, ending on a loop row. Now, leaving the loops just worked on the hook, insert the hook into the edge stitch 2 rows below, wind yarn over hook and draw a loop through, wind yarn over hook and draw through the first loop on hook, work slip stitches down the side of the buttonhole.

3 Now insert the hook into the first of the group of vertical loops that have been left unworked. Wind the yarn over the hook and draw a loop through —two loops on the hook.

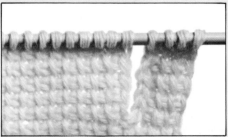

4 Continue across these unworked stitches to the end of the row. Work the same number of rows on these stitches as those on the other side of the buttonhole, ending with a loop row.

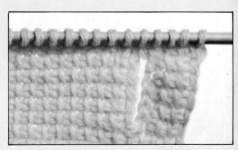

5 Re-join the row by working a return row over all the loops on the hook, making sure that there are the same number of loops as before. This completes the buttonhole.

Bobbles

Bobbles give fabric an attractive embossed texture and can be worked between stitches or on top of the fabric. Chain bobbles, worked between stitches, are made with three or four chain stitches, which are added in the return row. Double crochet bobbles are made on top of the fabric by working several times into one stitch.

Larger bobbles can be used not only to make a heavily textured fabric, which looks especially attractive if you use a bulky yarn, but they can also be incorporated into the main fabric as decorative buttons.

Chain bobbles

1 Work across the return row from left to right to the position of the bobble. Work three chain stitches.

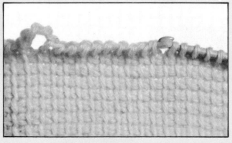

2 Then continue the return row, drawing the yarn through two loops at a time.

3 On the next loop row make loops into the vertical loops in the row below. When you reach the extra chains keep them to the front of the work.

4 A bobbled fabric can be made by placing bobbles after every fourth stitch in a row, working three rows plain and then altering the position of the bobbles so that they lie between the previous ones.

5 Bobbles made of four chains are shown here worked on Tunisian stockinette stitch.

6 Bobbles made of four chains are shown here worked on Tunisian purl stitch.

Double crochet bobbles

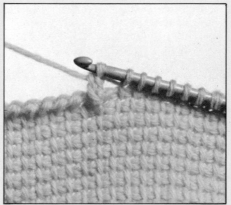

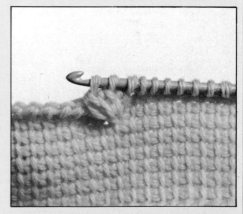

1 On a loop row work to the position of the bobble. Wind the yarn over the hook and insert the hook into the vertical loop *below* the next vertical loop.

2 Wind the yarn over the hook and draw a loop through. Wind the yarn over the hook and draw through the first two loops on the hook.

3 Make two more doubles into the same vertical loop.

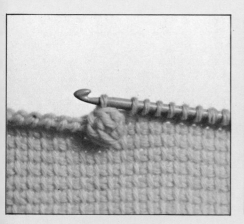

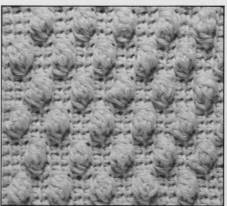

4 Now wind the yarn over the hook and draw through the first three loops on the hook. This completes the double crochet bobble. If you are using a fine yarn you may find that 4 doubles instead of 3 make a rounder bobble.

5 A bobbled fabric can be made by making bobbles into every 4th stitch in a row, working three rows plain and then altering the position of the bobbles, so that they lie between the previous ones.

6 To make a bobble button with the main fabric, work to position of button, then work 4dc all into next loop, leaving the last loop of each dc on the hook, yo and draw a loop through first 4 loops on hook, patt to end of row.

Fred Mancini

19

Stitch Wise

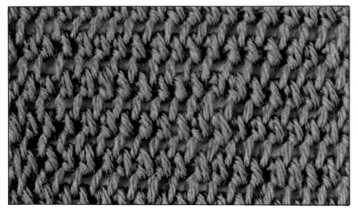 

Tunisian double crochet

Make a length of chains.
1st row Yo and insert hook into 3rd ch from hook, yo and draw a loop through, yo and draw through 2 loops on hook, *yo and insert hook into next ch, yo and draw a loop through, yo and draw through 2 loops on hook, rep from * to end. Do not turn work.
2nd row Yo and draw through first loop on hook, *yo and draw through 2 loops on hook, rep from * to end. Do not turn work.
3rd row 2ch, yo and insert hook into 2nd vertical loop in row below, yo and draw a loop through, yo and draw through 2 loops on hook, *yo and insert hook into next vertical loop below, yo and draw a loop through, yo and draw

through 2 loops on hook, rep from * to end. Do not turn work.
The 2nd and 3rd rows form the patt and are rep throughout.

Tunisian brick stitch

Make a length of chains.
1st row Insert hook into 2nd ch from hook, yo and draw a loop through, *insert hook into next ch, yo and draw a loop through, rep from * to end. Do not turn work.
2nd row Yo and draw through first loop on hook, *yo and draw through 2 loops on hook, rep from * to end. Do not turn work.
3rd row Insert hook from front to back under ch between first 2 vertical loops in row below, yo and draw a loop

through, *insert hook under ch between next 2 vertical loops, yo and draw a loop through, rep from * to last 2 vertical loops, skip space between these 2 loops and insert hook into vertical edge st, yo and draw a loop through. Do not turn work.
4th row As 2nd.
5th row Skip space between first and 2nd vertical loops and insert hook from front to back under ch between 2nd and 3rd vertical loops, yo and draw a loop through, *insert hook under ch between next 2 vertical loops, yo and draw a loop through, rep from * to end working into each space between sts including space between last 2 vertical loops, then insert hook into vertical edge st, yo and draw a loop through. Do not turn work.
Rows 2–5 form the patt and are rep throughout.

Baby cardigans

Two cardigans, one in white, one in variegated yarn, to crochet for a young baby.

Variegated cardigan

Sizes
To fit 16[18:20]in (41[46:51]cm) chest
Length, 6¾[8:9]in (17[20:23]cm).
Sleeve seam, 4½[5¼:6]in (11[12:14]cm).
Note: Directions for larger sizes are in brackets []; if there is only one set of figures it applies to all sizes.

Materials
3[4:5]oz (60[80:100]g) of a variegated sport yarn
Size F (4.00mm) Tunisian crochet hook
Size C (3.00mm) crochet hook
4[4:5] buttons

Gauge
24 sts and 44 rows (22 vertical loops) to 4in (10cm) worked on size F (4.00mm) Tunisian hook.

Back
Using size F (4.00mm) Tunisian hook make 53[61:69] ch.
**Base row *Insert hook into top loop of next ch, yo and draw a loop through, rep from * to end. Do not turn work.
53[61:69] loops.
Next row Yo and draw a loop through first loop on hook, *yo and draw through next 2 loops on hook, rep from * to end.
Beg patt.
1st row *Insert hook under next vertical loop from right to left and draw a loop through, rep from * to end.
Do not turn work. 53[61:69] loops.
2nd row Yo and draw a loop through first loop on hook, yo and draw through next 2 loops on hook, rep from * to end.
3rd and 4th rows As first and 2nd.
5th row Work 1 vertical loop, yo and insert hook under vertical loop *below* next vertical loop, yo and draw loop through, yo and draw through first 2 loops on hook, (yo and insert hook under same vertical loop, yo and draw a loop through, yo and draw through first 2 loops on hook) twice, yo and draw through first 3 loops on hook — called make bobble or MB — , work * 3 vertical loops, MB, rep

from * to within last 2 vertical loops, work 2 vertical loops. Do not turn work.
6th row As 2nd.
7th to 14th rows Rep first and 2nd rows 4 times.
15th row As 5th.
16th row As 2nd.
17th to 24th rows Rep first and 2nd rows 4 times.
25th row As 5th.
26th row As 2nd.
Cont in plain Tunisian st (rep rows 1 and 2) until work measures 2½[3¼:4]in (6[8:10]cm); end with a loop row. ******
Shape raglan
1st and 2nd rows Work next 2 vertical loops tog to dec one loop, work to within last 3 vertical loops, work next 2 vertical loops tog to dec one loop, work 1 vertical loop, then work back. Rep these 2 rows until 17[19:21] loops rem.
Work a loop row and a return row without shaping.
Fasten off.

Left front
Using size F (4.00mm) Tunisian hook make 25 [29:33] ch.
Work as for back from ** to **.

Shape raglan and front edge

1st and 2nd rows Work next two vertical loops tog to dec one loop, work to within last 3 vertical loops, work next 2 loops tog to dec one loop, work 1 vertical loop, then work back.

3rd and 4th rows Work next 2 vertical loops tog, work to end, then work back.

5th to 6th rows As 3rd-4th rows. Rep last 6 rows 4[5:6] times more. Then dec at raglan edge only until 2 loops rem.

Fasten off.

Right front

Work to match left front reversing all shaping.

Sleeves

Using size F (4.00mm) Tunisian hook make 29[33:37] ch. Work base row and next row as for back, then work patt rows 1 to 5.

Cont in plain Tunisian st (rep rows 1 and 2), inc one loop (see page 4) at each end of next and every foll 4th loop row until there are 43[49:55] loops, then work back.

Work straight to 4[4¾:5½]in (10[12:14]cm) from beg.

Shape raglan

Work the 2 rows of back raglan until 7 loops rem. Work a loop row and a return row without shaping.
Fasten off.

To finish

Join raglan seams, then join side and sleeve seams. For cuffs work 5 rounds of sc as for white cardigan.

Lower border

With RS facing join yarn to lower edge of left front and using size C (3.00mm) crochet hook work a row of sc evenly all around lower edge. Turn. Work 7 rows in sc. Fasten off.

Front border

With RS facing join yarn to lower edge of right front and using size C (3.00mm) crochet hook work 25 [29:33] sc along front edge to beg of front shaping, 67[70:73] sc evenly up right front, around back neck and 25[29:33] sc along front to lower edge.

Work 1 row in sc, down left front to beg of shaping and so ending at lower edge of right front.

1st buttonhole row 1 sc into each of first 2sc, (2ch. skip next 2sc, 1sc into each of next 5[6:5] sc) 3[3:4] times, 2ch, skip next 2sc, 1sc into each sc to end. Turn.

2nd Buttonhole row 1 sc into each sc and 2sc into each space to end. Turn.

Work 1 row in sc.

Fasten off.

Sew on buttons.

White cardigan

Sizes

To fit 16[18]in (41[46]cm chest.
Length, 7[8½]in (17.5[19]cm).
Sleeve, 6[6¾]in (15[17]cm).

Note: Directions for larger size are in brackets [ ]; if there is only one set of figures it applies to both sizes.

Materials

5[6]oz (120[140]g) of a sport yarn
Size F (4.00mm) Tunisian crochet
   hook
Size C (3.00mm) crochet hook
5 buttons

Gauge

24 sts and 44 rows (22 vertical loops) to 4in (10cm) worked on size F (4.00mm) Tunisian hook.

Left side

**Using size F (4.00mm) Tunisian hook make 29[37] ch for lower edge of sleeve. Cont in plain Tunisian st (see Volume 14, page 21) inc one loop (see page 4) at each end of foll 2 alternate loop rows. Work a loop row and a return row without shaping.

Bobble row Inc one loop, then work 1 vertical loop, yo and insert hook under vertical loop *below* next vertical loop, yo and draw a loop through, yo and draw through first 2 loops on hook, (yo and insert hook under same vertical loop, yo and draw a loop through, yo and draw through first 2 loops on hook) twice, yo and draw through first 3 loops on hook — called make bobble or MB—, work * 3 vertical loops, MB, rep from * to within last 2 vertical loops, work one vertical

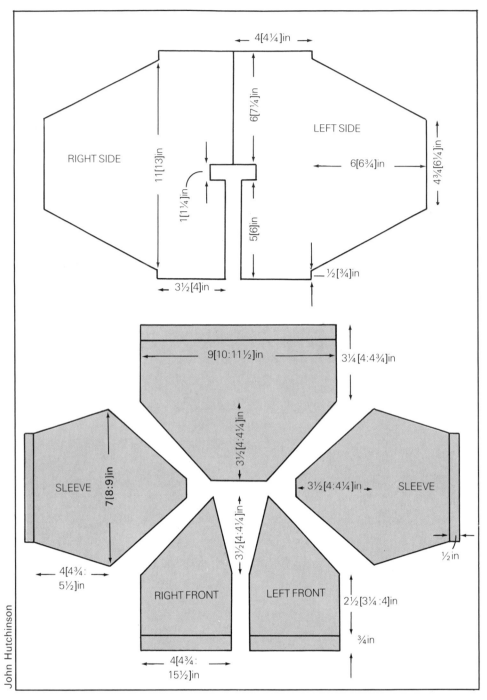

With RS facing skip next 7[9] loops, join yarn to next loop and work loops to end, then work back. 30[36] loops. Work 3 loop rows, working a bobble row on 3rd of these rows.
Fasten off.

Right side
Work as left side from ** to **
Shape neck
Next row Work until there are 30[35] loops on hook, then work back. Work 3 loop rows, working a bobble row on 3 of these rows. Fasten off.
With RS of work facing skip next 7[9] loops, join yarn to next loop and work loops to end, then work back. 36[44] loops. Work 5 loop rows, working a bobble row on 3rd of these rows.
Next row Work 1 sc into each vertical loop to end.
Fasten off.

To finish
With WS of pieces tog, using size C (3.00mm) crochet hook and working through the double thickness, join center back seam working 1 sc into each sc. With WS of pieces tog, using size C (3.00mm) crochet hook and working through the double thickness, work a row of sc evenly along side and sleeve edges.

Lower border
With RS facing join on yarn and using size C (3.00mm) crochet hook work 1 sc into each row end along lower edge.
Turn. Work 8 rows sc.
Fasten off.

Front border
With RS facing join yarn to lower edge of right front and using size C (3.00mm) crochet hook work 37[42] sc evenly along front edge to neck, 3sc into corner, 44[48] sc evenly around neck, 3sc into corner, then 37[42] sc along front to lower edge. Turn.
Work 2 rows sc, working 3sc into sc at corners.
1st buttonhole row 1 sc into each of first 2sc, 2ch, skip next 2sc, *1sc into each of next 6[7]sc, 2ch, skip next 2sc, rep from * 3 times more, 1sc into each sc to corner, 1sc into each sc to next corner, 3sc into corner, 1sc into each sc to end. Turn.
2nd buttonhole row Work 1sc into each sc and 2sc into each buttonhole. Turn.
Work 1 row sc. Fasten off.

Sleeve borders (alike)
With RS facing join on yarn and using size C (3.00mm) crochet hook work 1sc into each foundation ch along lower edge.
Next round 1 sc into each sc all around, sl st into first sc.
Rep last round once more.
Fasten off.
Sew on buttons.

loop, inc one loop, 1 vertical loop. Do not turn work. 35[43] loops. Work in plain Tunisian st, inc one loop at each end of foll 2 alternate loop rows, then work a loop row and a return row without shaping. Cont in this way, working extra loops into bobble patt and alternating bobbles, inc one loop at each end of every other loop row and working bobbles on first [2nd] loop row and every foll 6th [7th] loop row until 5 bobble rows have been worked and there are 59[71] vertical loops. Work a loop row and a return row without shaping. Inc one loop at each end of next 3 loop rows and work a bobble row on 3rd loop row. 65[77] vertical loops. This completes sleeve.
Using a separate ball of yarn make 4ch and leave aside.
Next row 4[6] ch, work a loop into top loop only of each of the next 3[5]ch, work a loop row to end, then work a loop into top loop only of each of the 4[6] ch. Do not turn the work. 73[89] loops. Cont in plain Tunisian st without shaping and working bobbles on 3rd loop row then on every foll 4th loop row until 4[5] bobble rows have been worked from completion of sleeve.**
Shape neck
Next row Work until there are 36[44] loops on hook, then work back. Work 5 loop rows, working a bobble row on 3rd of these rows.
Next row Work 1 sc into each vertical loop to end. Fasten off.

John Hutchinson

Crochet / COURSE 69

*Crochet on canvas
*Working chains on canvas
*Crochet squares worked on canvas
*Ways of joining canvas
*Two patterns for crochet canvas bags

Crochet on canvas

This interesting and unusual technique is very quick and easy to work and is ideal for making wool rugs, mats, belts and bags in a variety of patterns.

Evenweave canvas with 14 squares to 2in (5cm), ordinary rug canvas with 7 squares to 2in (5cm) and quick needlepoint canvas with 9½ squares to 2in (5cm) can all be used. The canvas is available from most craft shops and needlework departments in a variety of widths.

Ordinary rug canvas is the easiest to use,

since the holes are fairly large and can be used with a bulky, Aran or knitting worsted yarn, using two strands together when necessary. The finer evenweave canvas and quick needlepoint canvas should be used for more intricate patterns with a knitting worsted or sport yarn, used double if necessary.

The hook must be small enough to pass easily through the holes in the canvas, but not so small that it cannot draw the yarn through.

If the canvas is fairly stiff, you should be able to crochet on it without the use of an embroidery frame, although if a large piece is to be worked, you may find it easier to work with a frame, moving it across the canvas when necessary.

Once you are familiar with the technique, try experimenting with different materials, including jute, thick parcel string, raffia and various kinds of knitting yarns to see the many different effects that can be achieved.

Working chains on canvas

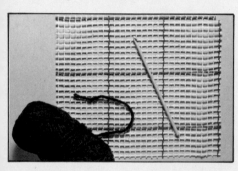

1 Use rug canvas such as the sample shown here with a thick yarn and medium-size hook (size H [5.00mm] would be ideal) for large items and bold patterns.

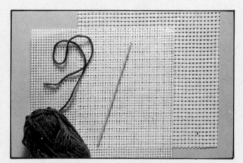

2 Quick needlepoint canvas shown on right and evenweave canvas shown on left are both suitable when working intricate patterns. Use knitting worsted or a 4-ply sport yarn and size B (2.50mm) hook for best results.

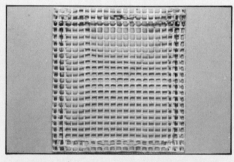

3 Use of a square of rug canvas and bulky yarn to work this sample. Take a piece of rug canvas approximately 8in (20cm) square and turn back at least 2 rows all around. Baste around edge as shown here to hold edges in place.

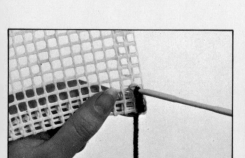

4 With RS facing, hold yarn behind canvas. Insert the hook into the bottom right-hand corner, through all thicknesses, and draw a loop of yarn through to the RS. Wind yarn over hook and draw it through loop on hook.

5 Keeping yarn at back of canvas, insert hook into next hole above previous stitch and draw yarn through. Now draw yarn through loop on hook to make chain stitch. Do not pull yarn tightly or you may pull canvas out of shape.

6 Continue working a chain stitch into each hole to the top of the canvas, working through the double thickness. Do not turn. Insert hook into the hole on the left, adjacent to last stitch, and work one stitch.

continued

Fred Mancini

7 Now turn canvas and continue to work back down canvas to lower edge, working through double thickness as before. Work one chain into the hole on the right, adjacent to last stitch, as before.

8 Turn canvas. Work each row in same way, using a variety of colors for a simple striped pattern. I o make stitches all run the same way, break off yarn at top of work and start each row from the lower edge.

9 For a longer, flatter stitch insert the hook into every other hole up the canvas, extending the yarn each time to cover canvas completely. Although stitches are worked vertically they can be used horizontally.

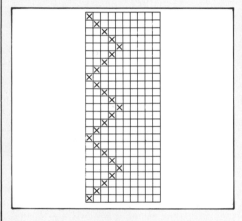

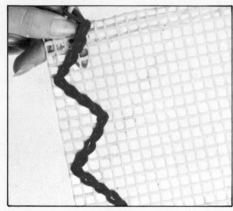

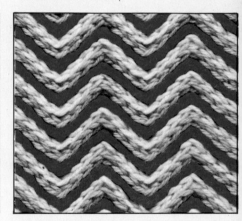

10 To make a zig-zag pattern, plan the first line of the pattern on graph paper as shown here, using each square to represent a square on the canvas.

11 Work the first row of chain stitches from the chart at the edge of the work to act as a guide. Move stitches up one row and to the right for required number of stitches, then up one square and to left for the same number of squares.

12 The 2nd and following rows are then worked beside the first until the canvas has been completely covered. Fill in unworked squares at side edges. Although the pattern is worked vertically it can be used horizontally as shown here.

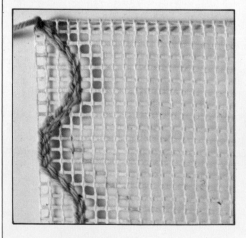

13 For a more curved effect, work two or three stitches straight, curving the line up or down as shown.

14 Once the guide line has been completed, continue to work the pattern following the guide line until all holes have been covered.

15 Fill in the holes left unworked at each side, starting each row in same hole as previous row to ensure complete coverage of canvas.

Crochet squares on canvas

Canvas squares make ideal rugs, cushions and mats since several can be worked and then sewn together on the wrong side. The chain stitches are worked on the canvas using the same technique as before, but working from the center outward in rounds. Once the squares have been completed all the loose ends must be darned into the wrong side before the squares are sewn together.

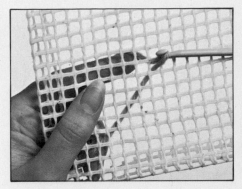

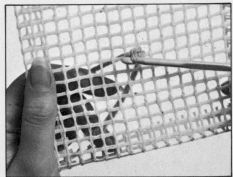

1 Cut a square of canvas the required size. Don't forget to allow at least 2 rows extra around for turning under. Hold yarn at back of work. Now insert hook into one of the center 4 squares and draw through a loop.

2 Insert hook into next hole to left and draw yarn through, then through loop on hook to make first chain stitch and hold yarn in place.

3 Work chain stitches around remaining center squares to form center group. Now insert hook into next hole up and make one chain stitch to start next round.

4 Continue to crochet around center group, turning canvas at corners so that you are always working in same direction. To change color, drop old yarn at back of work and draw new yarn through to complete stitch.

5 Insert hook into next square up to start next round. Continue working in rounds in this way, changing colors as required and working through double thickness at outer edge to complete the square.

Ways of joining canvas

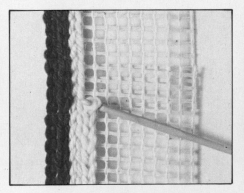

1 To sew several squares together, darn all loose ends into wrong side as neatly as possible. Then overcast canvas squares together, using two strands either of the same yarn or of a matching yarn in a finer ply.

2 When making a long strip where two pieces are needed to achieve the length required, lay the canvas being worked over the new piece of canvas and work through double thickness.

3 Continue to work in pattern, working through both thicknesses of canvas where they meet to achieve a neat joining as shown here. (The wrong side is shown in the top photograph.)

Fred Mancini

Rod Delroy

26

Canvas bags

Once you've practiced crochet on canvas for a little while, you'll find this stylish purse and handy shopping bag in warm shades of plum and brown very easy.

Please note that the dimensions of canvas given in the following patterns are approximate only. Canvas is not exactly square, so you should check that you have the exact number of holes specified after turning the hems.

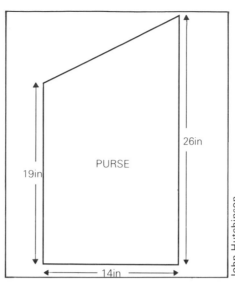

PURSE

19in 26in 14in

John Hutchinson

Purse

Size
12 × 8in (30 × 21cm).

Materials
3oz (60g) of a sport yarn in main color (A)
1oz (20g) in contrasting color (B)
Size B (2.50mm) crochet hook
20in (50cm) of 36in (90cm)-wide evenweave canvas with 14 holes to 2in (5cm)
⅝yd (.5m) of cotton fabric for lining

To make
Cut a piece of canvas foll measurements on diagram. Turn approx. 1in (2.5cm) to WS all around canvas, leaving 89 holes along lower edge, 126 holes along short side edge and 170 holes along long side edge to be worked. Cut away corners so that hem lies flat, then baste hem in place. Using size B (2.50mm) hook and A, beg at lower right-hand corner of canvas work in basic chain st into every other hole for 118 rows, then foll chart at bottom of page 28 from row 119 following arrows to row 162. Fasten off. Using size B (2.50mm) hook and B, beg at point indicated on chart, work border, working basic chain st into every hole. Fasten off. Darn in all ends.

To finish
Cut lining to fit. Overcast to WS of bag. Fold 16in (41cm) from lower edge in half. Join side seams. Turn down flap.

Shopping bag

Size
14in (36cm) square.

Materials
4oz (80g) of a sport yarn in 1st color (A)
4oz (80g) in 2nd color (B)
4oz (80g) in 3rd color (C)
Size B (2.50mm) crochet hook
1yd (1m) of 36in (90cm)-wide evenweave canvas with 14 holes to 2in (5cm)
1yd (1m) of cotton fabric for lining

To make
Cut two pieces of canvas 18¼in (46.5cm) × 18¾in (47.5cm) long for back and front. Turn approx. 1in (2.5cm) to WS all around canvas, leaving 100 holes by 104 holes to be worked. Cut away corners so that hem lies flat, then baste hem in place. From rem canvas cut two strips, each 6 × 33½in (15 × 85cm), for handle and gusset. Turn 1in (2.5cm) to WS around outer edge of each strip, then baste hem in place. Using size B (2.50mm) hook and A, beg at lower right-hand corner of canvas, foll chart overleaf work in basic chain st into each hole and working each section

until all holes of each shape are filled. Fasten off. Darn in all ends. Using size B (2.50mm) hook and B, beg at lower right-hand corner of one strip, work in basic chain st working in stripes of 9 rows B, (18 rows C, 18 rows A) twice, 18 rows C, *18 rows B, 18 rows C, 18 rows A, rep from * 5 times more, joining strips when necessary (see page 25), then work 9 rows B. Fasten off.

To finish

Overcast gusset and handle to lower edge and sides of bag, leaving remainder free for handle. Cut lining to fit, then overcast lining to inside of bag.

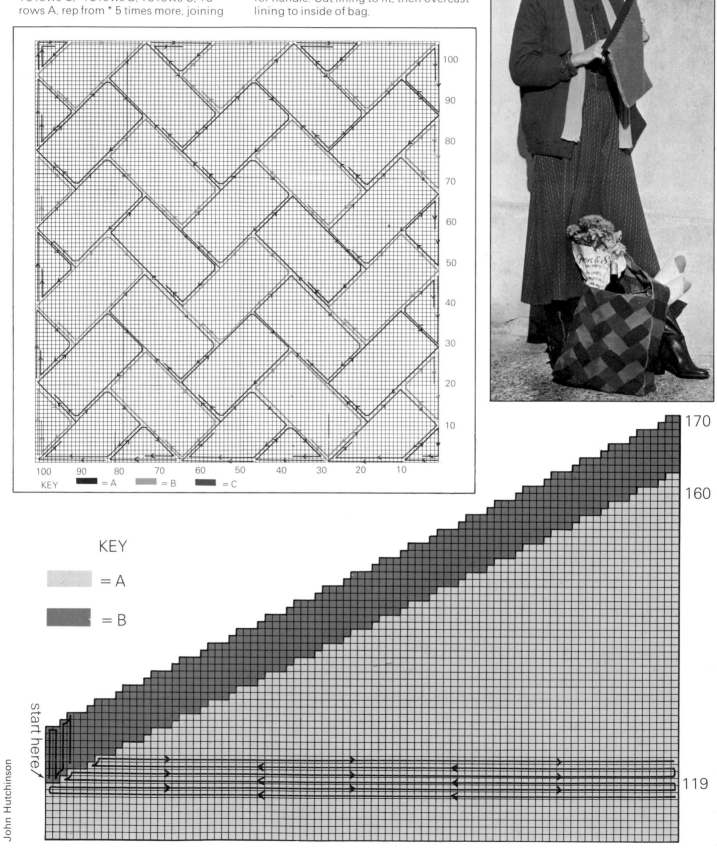

100
90
80
70
60
50
40
30
20
10

100 90 80 70 60 50 40 30 20 10
KEY ■ = A ▨ = B ▨ = C

170
160
119

KEY

□ = A

■ = B

start here

John Hutchinson

*Working a neckline with lapels
*Working a separate collar with lapels
*Pattern for a boy's jacket

Working a neckline with lapels

A lapel is the turned-back edge of a neckline, displaying a triangular section of lining. The total look of this tailored neckline is completed by a separate collar—the short ends of the collar are either partially or completely attached to the top of the lapel.

The following step-by-step instructions describe how to make the lapels of the boy's jacket on page 32. This is the traditional method of making this type of collar on a stockinette stitch garment where the facing of the lapel is knitted and shaped with the front.

The finishing of the collar requires some dressmaking skills to produce a professional look on the finished garment.

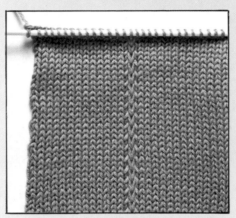

1 The front edges of a stockinette stitch garment must have a knitted facing below the neckline. After knitting the hem, cast on extra stitches at the front edge for the facing. Mark the front edge by working a slip stitch on knit rows only. This gives a distinctive line of stitches and a neat foldline for the facing.

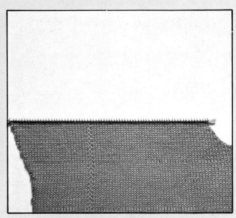

2 The facing is shaped so that when the lapel is folded back, this stockinette stitch section is uppermost. Shaping—by increasing one stitch at the edge of the facing at regular intervals—begins before the armhole shaping. Continue to increase at the facing edge throughout the armhole shaping. This is how the front looks after the armhole shaping is complete.

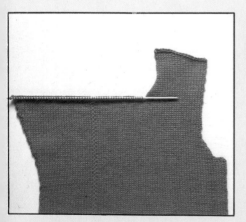

3 Follow the pattern and work the necessary amount of shaping at the facing edge only. Leave the lapels and facing stitches on a spare needle or holder while shaping the front neck and completing the shoulder.

4 Rejoin the yarn to the inner edge of the stitches on the spare needle and bind off a number of stitches—equal on each side of the foldline—to represent the lapel edge on the front and facing. Still increasing at the outer edge, shape the neck edge and shoulder of the facing to correspond with the front. Note that the shoulder edge of the facing is only about two-thirds as wide as the front shoulder to fit part of the way along shoulder line.

5 Make a separate collar according to the instructions given in the pattern. This shape is folded in half at the marked line to form a double collar: the straight, cast-on and bound-off edges fit along the back neck, while the shaped edge fits along the front neck.

continued

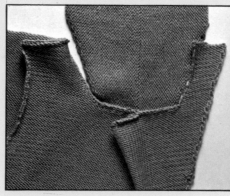

6 After joining the shoulder seams, assemble the collar and lapels. With right sides of the fabric together, turn back facing at foldline. Join half of lapel edge: here it is joined with contrasting-colored yarn for clarity.

7 Turn facing right side out. Join ends of collar to remaining edges of lapels. With right sides together, sew upper collar to facing and under collar to front.

8 With right sides together, sew under collar in place along front and back neck edges, placing middle of collar at center back neck edge. Also join shaped edge of upper collar to neck shaping or facing.

9 Fold collar in half at turning line and slip stitch upper side of collar in place along back neck.

10 Check that front facings are folded in half to wrong side of work. Finish the facings on the wrong side by slip stitching edge of front and lapel facings in place, joining shaped top of facing to shoulder line.

11 Fold the collar and lapel back onto the right side of the garment, making sure that the edge of the facing is well hidden. The finished collar must look neat and well-tailored.

Working a separate collar with lapels

You can add this type of collar to most V-necklines, whether they are on a sweater, cardigan or jacket. Use it to replace the original neckband, borders or collar given in a pattern, or give an old garment an up-to-date look with a new collar.

This version of a collar with lapels is ideal for working in seed stitch or garter stitch. Both stitches make a neat collar that needs no facing. Note that the stitches on the top part of the collar and those on the lapel lie in different directions; if you want them both in the same direction, knit the top collar with the short ends as the cast-on and bound-off edges.

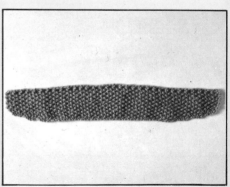

1 Join the shoulder seams of the garment with a V neckline—it may be a jacket or sweater, as here. Don't work a neckline or any other finish around the neck.

2 Make a collar in seed stitch (see Volume 14, page 51). The collar is shaped at the cast-on edge to come the required distance down the front neck. The narrow ends of the collar are usually about half the top width of the triangular lapel (see step 4).

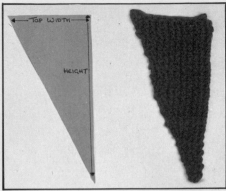

3 Sew collar in place around back neck and down sides of front neck. Here the lapel part of the collar is represented in cut-out paper: before being turned back, it is usually half the V shape of the neckline below the collar already sewn on.

4 Measure the top width and height of the paper collar. Using your seed stitch gauge, calculate the number of rows in height and stitches in the top width. Start with two stitches and increase at one edge only at regular intervals to required triangular shape.

5 Sew right side of shaped edge of lapels to wrong side of remaining neckline. With right sides of fabric together, join short ends of collar to lapel. Turn collar back onto the front of the garment.

Boy's jacket

Any boy will be pleased with this stylish jacket with its shiny buttons.

Sizes
To fit 30[32:34]in (77[83:87]cm) chest. Length, 21¾[22½:23½]in (55[57:60]cm). Sleeve seam, 14½[15½:16½]in (36[39:42]cm).
Note: Directions for the larger sizes are in brackets []; if there is only one set of figures it applies to all sizes.

Materials
22[24:24]oz (600[650:650]g) of a knitting worsted
1 pair each Nos. 5 and 6 (4 and 4½mm) knitting needles
10 buttons; stitch holder

Gauge
22 sts and 30 rows to 4in (10cm) in stockinette st on No. 6 (4½mm) needles.

Back
Using No. 5 (4mm) needles cast on 30[32:34] sts for right side of vent. Beg with a K row, work 7 rows stockinette st.
Next row K into back of each st to mark hem line. **
Change to No. 6 (4½mm) needles.
1st row K to end.
2nd row K2, P to end.
Rep these 2 rows 18[19:20] times more, then work 1st row again.
Next row Bind off 6 sts, P to end. Leave rem 24[26:28] sts on a holder. Using No. 5 (4mm) needles cast on 30[32:34] sts for left side of vent. Work as for right side to **. Change to No. 6 (4½mm) needles.
1st row K to end.
2nd row P to last 2 sts, K2.
Rep these 2 rows 18[19:20] times more, then work first row again.
Next row P to last 6 sts, bind off 6 sts. Leave rem 24[26:28] sts on a holder. Using No. 5 (4mm) needles cast on 26[28:30] sts for flap. Beg with a K row, work 7 rows stockinette st, inc one st at each end of every row. 40[42:44] sts.
Next row K into back of each st to mark hemline.
Change to No. 6 (4½mm) needles.
1st row Inc in first st, K to last st, inc in last st.
2nd row Inc in first st, P to last st, inc in last st.
3rd row Inc in first st, sl 1 purlwise, K to last 2 sts, sl 1, inc in last st.
4th row As 2nd.
5th row Inc in first st, K2, sl 1, K to last 4 sts, sl 1, K2, inc in last st.
6th row As 2nd.
7th row Inc in first st, K4, sl 1, K to last 6 sts, sl 1, K4, inc in last st.
8th row P to end. 54[56:58] sts. Beg with a K row, cont in stockinette st for 31[33:35] rows, keeping sl sts correct.
Next row Bind off 7 sts, P to last 7 sts, bind off these 7 sts. 40[42:44] sts.
Join sides of vent and flap
Next row K across right vent sts on holder, K across flap sts, then K across left vent sts on holder. 88[94:100] sts. Beg with a P row, cont in stockinette st until work measures 15[15½:16]in (38[39:41]cm) from hemline; end with a P row.
Shape armholes
Bind off 4 sts at beg of next 2 rows. Dec one st at each end of next and every foll alternate row until 70[74:78] sts rem. Cont straight until armholes measure 6¾[7:7½]in (17[18:19]cm); end with a P row.
Shape shoulders
Bind off 6[7:7] sts at beg of next 4 rows and 7[6:7] sts at beg of foll 2 rows. Bind off rem 32[34:36] sts.

Left front
Using No. 6 (4½mm) needles cast on 20[22:22] sts for pocket lining. Beg with a K row, work 8 rows stockinette st. Cut off yarn and leave sts on a holder. Using No. 5 (4mm) needles cast on 54[57:60] sts. Work 7 rows stockinette st, beg with a K row.
Next row Cast on 21 sts, K into back of each st to mark hemline. 75[78:81] sts. Change to No. 6 (4½mm) needles.
1st row K to last 21 sts, sl 1, K20.
2nd row P to end.
Rep these 2 rows 14 times more.
Divide for pocket
Next row K14[15:18], leave rem sts on a holder, then K across 20[22:22] sts of pocket lining. 34[37:40] sts. Beg with a P row, work 30 rows stockinette st.
Next row Bind off 20[22:22] sts, P to end. Do not break off yarn.
Return to sts on holder, rejoin new ball of yarn and work as foll:
1st buttonhole row K23[25:25], bind off 3 sts, K7, bind off 3 sts, K4, sl 1, K3, bind off 3 sts, K7, bind off 3 sts, K to end.
2nd buttonhole row P to end, casting on 3 sts over those bound off in previous row. Beg with a K row, work 30 rows stockinette st, keeping sl st correct. Cut off yarn. Working across both groups of sts, work 2 more buttonholes as foll:
1st buttonhole row K37[40:43], bind off

3 sts, K7, bind off 3 sts, K4, sl 1, K3, bind off 3 sts, K7, bind off 3 sts, K to end.

2nd buttonhole row P to end, casting on 3 sts over those bound off in previous row. *** Beg with a K row, work 30 rows stockinette st across all sts, keeping sl st correct. Work 2 more buttonhole rows.

Shape facing

Inc one st at facing edge on next and every foll 4th row until front measures same as back to underarm; end at side edge.

Shape armhole

Cont to inc at facing edge as before, bind off 4 sts at beg of next row.

Dec one st at armhole edge on foll 5[6:7] alternate rows.

Keeping armhole edge straight, cont to inc at facing edge until there are 78[81:84] sts. Work 1 row, so ending at armhole edge.

Shape neck

Next row Work 24[27:30] sts, turn and leave rem sts on a holder.

Dec one st at neck edge on foll 5[7:9] alternate rows. Cont straight until front measures same as back to shoulders; end at armhole edge.

Shape shoulder

Bind off 6[7:7] sts at beg of next and foll alternate row. Work 1 row. Bind off rem 7[6:7] sts.

Rejoin yarn to rem sts, bind off 41 sts, work to end of row. Dec one st at neck edge on foll 5[7:7] alternate rows, *at the same time* inc at facing edge as before. Keeping neck straight, cont to inc at facing edge until there are 12[11:10] sts. Cont straight until facing measures same as front when folded at sl st; end at outer edge of facing.

Shape shoulder of facing

Bind off 5[5:3] sts at beg of next row. Work 1 row. Bind off rem 7[6:7] sts.

Right front

Using No. 6 (4½mm) needles cast on 20[22:22] sts. Work pocket lining as for left front. Using No. 5 (4mm) needles cast on 54[57:60] sts. Beg with a K row, work 6 rows stockinette st.

Next row Cast on 21 sts, K to end.

Next row K into back of each st to mark hemline.

Change to No. 6 (4½mm) needles.

1st row K20, sl 1, K to end.

2nd row P to end.

Rep these 2 rows 14 times more.

Divide for pocket

Next row K20, sl 1, K40[42:42], turn and leave rem sts on a holder.

P 1 row. Work 30 rows stockinette st, beg with a K row and keeping sl st correct. Leave sts on a holder. Do not cut off yarn.

Next row Using a new ball of yarn, K across sts of pocket lining, then across sts on first holder. 34[37:40] sts. Beg with a P row, work 30 rows stockinette st.

Next row P to last 20[22:22] sts, bind off these sts. Cut off yarn.

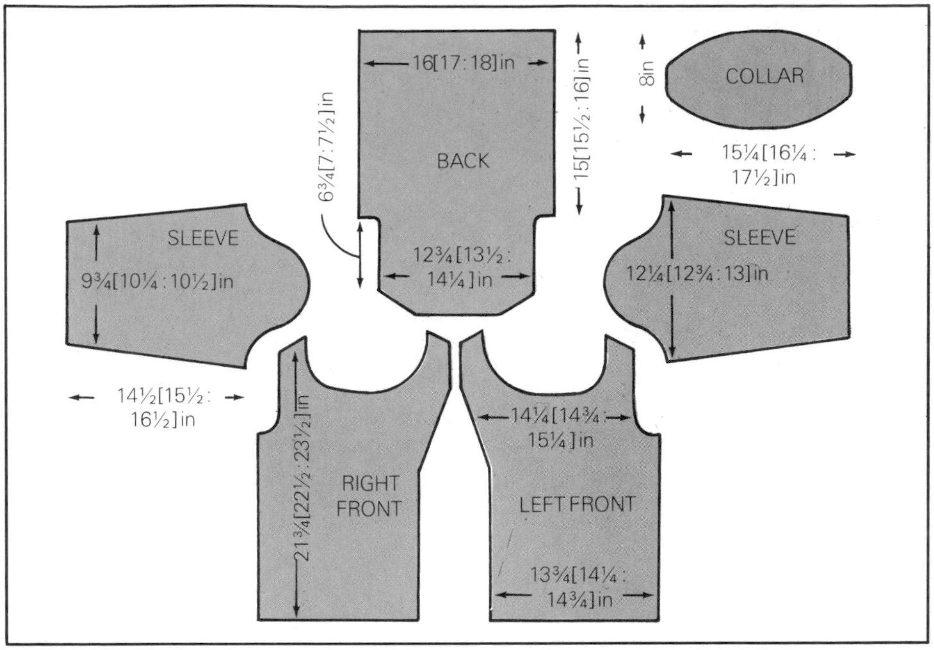

Return to sts on holder, K these sts, then rem sts. 75[78:81] sts. Complete as for left front from *** to end, omitting buttonholes and reversing shaping.

Sleeves

Using No. 5 (4mm) needles cast on 54[56:58] sts. Beg with a K row, work 7 rows stockinette st.

Next row K into back of each st to mark hemline.

Change to No. 6 (4½mm) needles. Beg with K row, cont in stockinette st, inc one st at each end of 11th[13th:15th] row and every foll 12th[14th:16th] row until there are 68[70:72] sts. Cont straight until sleeve measures 14½[15½:16½]in (36[39:42]cm) from hemline; end with a P row.

Shape top

Bind off 4 sts at beg of next 2 rows. Work 0[2:4] rows. Dec one st at each end of next and every other row until 36 sts rem, then at each end of every row until 26 sts rem. Bind off 3 sts at beg of next 4 rows.
Bind off rem 14 sts.

Sleeve trims (make 2)

Using No. 5 (4mm) needles cast on 14 sts.

1st row K3, sl 1, K6, sl 1, K3.

2nd row P to end.

Rep these 2 rows until trim measures 8in (20cm); end with a P row. Bind off.

Collar

Using No. 6 (4½mm) needles cast on 28[30:32] sts for upper collar. Beg with a K row, cont in stockinette st. Work 2 rows, then cast on 4 sts at beg of next 14[12:10] rows.

2nd and 3rd sizes only
Cast on 6 sts at beg of next 2[4] rows.

All sizes
Beg with a K row, work 15 rows stockinette st on these 84[90:96] sts. Change to No. 5 (4mm) needles.

Next row K into back of each st to mark turning line.

Beg with a K row, work 14 rows stockinette st for under collar.

2nd and 3rd sizes only
Bind off 6 sts at beg of next 2[4] rows.

All sizes
Bind off 4 sts at beg of next 14[12:10] rows. Bind off rem 28[30:32] sts.

Pocket trim

Using No. 5 (4mm) needles and with RS facing, pick up and K 26 sts along pocket. Beg with a P row, work 6 rows stockinette st.

Next row K into back of each st to mark turning line.

Beg with a K row, work 6 rows stockinette st. Bind off. Work trim on other pocket.

To finish

Press or block, according to yarn used. Join shoulder seams. Set in sleeves. Join side and sleeve seams. Turn back flap hems to WS, slip stitch in place and join mitered corners. Sew top of vents in place on WS. Turn hems at sleeves and lower edge to WS and slip stitch. Sew pocket linings in place. Fold pocket trims in half with RS tog and sew ends. Turn to RS, fold in half and slip stitch bound-off edge. Catch ends of trims down on RS. Fold sleeve trim at slip stitch lines with RS tog and sew ends. Turn to RS and bound-off edge to cast-on edge. Place trim on sleeve in position and secure by sewing a button at each end through all thicknesses. Assemble collar and lapels as shown in steps 6 to 11 on page 30. Catch down cast-on edge of facing at lower edge. Finish each set of buttonholes. Sew on buttons. Press seams and collar lightly.

Schematic diagram showing garment pieces: BACK (16[17:18]in wide, 15[15½:16]in, 6¾[7:7½]in, 12¾[13½:14¼]in), COLLAR (8in, 15¼[16¼:17½]in), two SLEEVE pieces (9¾[10¼:10½]in, 14½[15½:16½]in and 12¼[12¾:13]in), RIGHT FRONT (21¾[22½:23½]in), LEFT FRONT (14¼[14¾:15¼]in, 13¾[14¼:14¾]in).

John Hutchinson

*Introduction to patchwork knitting
*Working patches in strips
* Designing patchwork with squares and triangles
*Patterns for a patchwork baby blanket and child's sweater

Introduction to patchwork knitting

Patchwork knitting provides a fascinating exercise in color and texture. You can become your own designer and create individual designs based on a few simple techniques, colors and shapes.

In addition to designing your own fabrics, you can also use up scraps of yarn. Make sure they are a similar weight, and, if you intend to wash the garment, all the yarns must have similar laundering instructions. The main elements of a patchwork fabric are shape, color and texture. Shapes can be regular (squares, hexagons, diamonds, etc) or irregular, as in "crazy" patchwork; they can be made individually and sewn together later, or incorporated into one piece of knitting. Color often enhances the shapes and turns them into dazzling patterns.

More striking designs can be made with patchwork texture—using either various stitch patterns or different qualities of yarn such as tweed, mohair and bouclé. Texture patchworks are usually more difficult for an inexperienced knitter to create, because they involve various yarn thicknesses and complicated calculations with individual stitch gauges. The simplest solution is to use a combination of stockinette stitch and reverse stockinette stitch and different kinds of the same quality of yarn—for example, a plain and a Shetland-type knitting worsted.

Working patches in strips

You can easily design an individual random patchwork fabric by working strips of patches; this way there is no need to bind off after each patch and only the side edges of the strips need to be joined afterward.

This type of fabric usually looks best in stockinette stitch. Unless you have extremely good color sense, stick to a maximum of 4 or 5 colors.

Within individual patches, you can use a variety of techniques, such as narrow horizontal stripes, in which you carry the yarn up the side, narrow vertical stripes, in which the yarn is stranded across the back of the work, and wide vertical and diagonal stripes, which require small, separate balls of yarn. However, the fabric does not need to be too complex; a simple arrangement of stripes and plain patches in rich colors can be stunning.

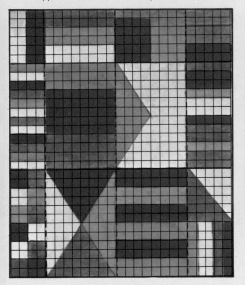

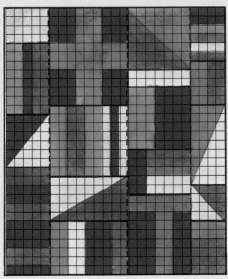

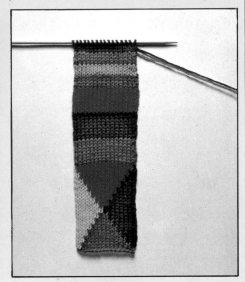

1 Decide on the finished size of the fabric that you want to make and draw it to scale (using squared or graph paper, if you like). Divide the width of the fabric into strips (which can be of different widths) and draw lines across them to make rectangles, as shown here. Color the scale drawing to show how you want the finished fabric to look.

2 Here the same measurements as in step 1 have been divided into an irregular arrangement of strips and patches. However, it's no more difficult to make than the first, as the patches in each strip are knitted without a break, using the same number of stitches.

3 First make a gauge sample in stockinette stitch and calculate the number of stitches you need to cast on for each strip of patches. Using your scale drawing as a guide, work all of the patches in one long strip.

Within each strip you may use a number of different techniques including those for narrow and wide horizontal, vertical and diagonal stripes.

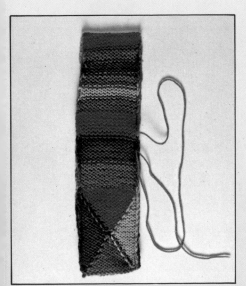

4 When the strips are finished, block and/or press them to size. Pin and baste the strips together to form a fabric before joining with neat overcasting stitches or a fine back stitch seam.

5 Press or block the finished fabric well according to the type of yarn used. On the right side of the work, the seams should be barely visible.

6 The wrong side must be neat; it is also a record of the various techniques you have used in making the patchwork.

Fred Mancini

Designing patchwork with squares and triangles

Many patchwork designs use square shapes, made separately and sewn together at a later stage. These squares are knitted—usually in stockinette or garter stitch—from corner to corner, increasing to form a triangular shape, then decreasing to complete the square. Turned at an angle of 45 degrees, the squares stand on one corner and can be used as a diamond shape.

Again, this type of patchwork fabric usually looks best in stockinette stitch and simple but striking color combinations.

There is an infinite number of designs you can make from these squares; some are shown below. Half squares (which are triangular because of the direction of the knitting) can be made to fill the angles of a fabric made up of diamond shapes.

Before you start knitting, spend some time working out arrangements of squares or diamonds on paper—it's a fascinating exercise in the basic principles of color and design.

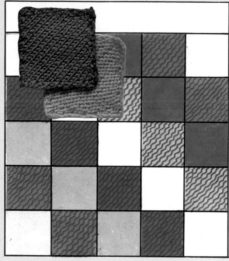

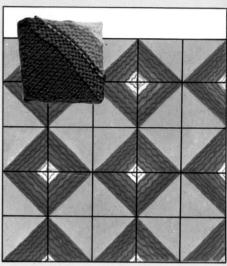

This square and triangle are made from the instructions for the baby blanket on page 37. One triangular section of the square is in stockinette stitch in one color and the other in reverse stockinette stitch in another color. Using reverse stockinette stitch increases the variety of patterns available.
Build up designs by altering the position of the reverse stockinette stitch section and using different colors.

This is a simple pattern of squares in four solid colors used in rotation in either stockinette stitch or reverse stockinette stitch alternately.

Each square (above) has been made with one triangular section in solid-color stockinette stitch and the remaining part in striped reverse stockinette stitch. The squares are positioned so that the triangular sections form large diamonds in the main fabric.

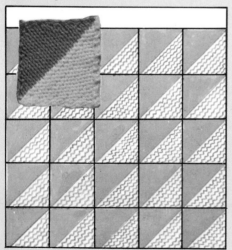

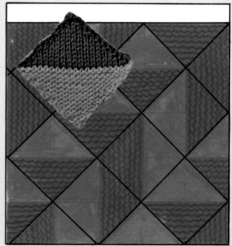

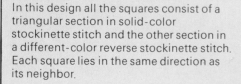

In this design all the squares consist of a triangular section in solid-color stockinette stitch and the other section in a different-color reverse stockinette stitch. Each square lies in the same direction as its neighbor.

Here, diamond shapes have been positioned so that the halves in one color of stockinette stitch are sewn together to form stripes, while the other halves make alternating triangular shapes in two colors.

This complicated-looking arrangement of diamonds uses only one basic square with half in one color of stockinette stitch and the other half in another color of reverse stockinette stitch.

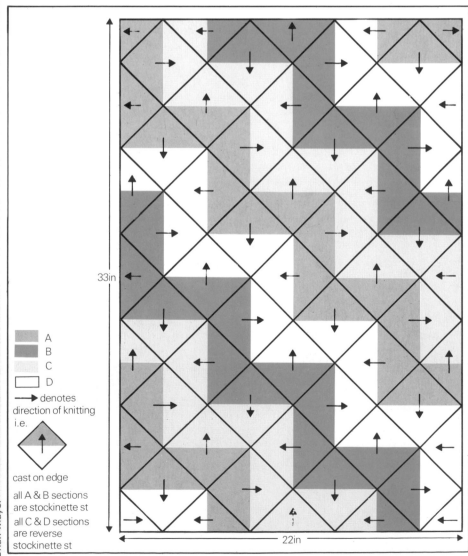

33in

22in

A
B
C
D

→ denotes direction of knitting i.e.

cast on edge

all A & B sections are stockinette st
all C & D sections are reverse stockinette st

Patchwork crib blanket

An ingenious arrangement of patchwork makes a pretty blanket for a new baby.

Size
33×22in (84×56cm).

Materials
5oz (120g) of a sport yarn in each of 4 colors (A, B, C and D)
Nos. 3 and 6 (3¼ and 4½mm) needles

Gauge
22 sts to 4in (10cm) in stockinette st on No. 6 (4½mm) needles. Each patch measures 4in (10cm) square.

Squares
Using No. 6 (4½mm) needles and A, cast on one st.
1st row (K1, P1, K1) into st.
2nd row P to end.
3rd row K into front and back of each of first 2 sts, K1.
4th row P into front and back of first st — called Pfb—, P to last 2 sts, Pfb, P1
5th row Kfb, K to last 2 sts, Kfb, K1.
6th and 7th rows As 2nd and 5th.
Rep 4th-7th rows 3 times more, then 4th and 5th rows again. **. 33 sts and 21 rows worked.
Cut off A. Join in C and P 2 rows (work is now in reverse stockinette st).
***24th row** K2 tog, K to last 2 sts, K 2 tog tbl.

25th row P2 tog tbl, P to last 2 sts, P2 tog.
26th row As 24th.
27th row P to end.
Rep 24th-27th rows 4 times more.
3 sts rem and 43 rows worked.
44th row Sl 1, K2 tog, psso and fasten off.
Make 10 squares in all using these 2 colors. Make 9 squares using A and D. Make 10 squares using B and C. Make 10 squares using B and D.

Triangles

First Using No. 6 ($4\frac{1}{2}$mm) needles and A, work as square to **. P1 row. Bind off. Make one more in A, then 2in B.
Second Using No. 6 ($4\frac{1}{2}$mm) needles and C, cast on 33 sts. P 1 row, then work as square from *** to end.
Make one more in C, then 2 in D.
Third Using No. 6 ($4\frac{1}{2}$mm) needles and A, cast on one st.
1st row (K1, P1) into st.
2nd row P2.
3rd row Kfb, K1.
4th row P1, Pfb, P1.
5th row Kfb, K to end.
6th row P to end.
Cont to inc at one side only until there are 17 sts and 21st row has been worked. Cut off A. Join in C and P 2 rows.
24th row K to last 2 sts, K2 tog tbl.
Cont to dec at this edge only to match square until 2 sts rem. K2 tog and fasten off. Make another triangle the same using A and D, one using B and C and one using B and D.
Fourth Using No. 6 ($4\frac{1}{2}$mm) needles and A, cast on one st. Work first 4 rows as 3rd triangle.
5th row K to last 2 sts, Kfb, K1.
6th row P to end.
7th row As 5th.
8th row Pfb, P to end.
Cont to match previous triangles, but reversing shaping. Make another using A and D, one using B and C and one using B and D.

Small triangles for corners

First Using No. 6 ($4\frac{1}{2}$mm) needles and A, work as first half of 4th triangle.
Second Using No. 6 ($4\frac{1}{2}$mm) needles and A, work as first half of 3rd triangle.
Third Using No. 6 ($4\frac{1}{2}$mm) needles and D, cast on 17 sts and work as second half of 3rd triangle.
Fourth Using No. 6 ($4\frac{1}{2}$mm) needles and D, cast on 17 sts and work as second half of 4th triangle.

To finish

Press or block pieces, according to yarn used. Join as shown in diagram, page 37.
Border
Using No. 3 ($3\frac{1}{4}$mm) needles and A, cast on 7 sts. Work in stockinette st, using colors to match blanket, working around all sides. Bind off. Sew on border, matching colors. Fold in half to WS and slip stitch.

Child's patchwork sweater

Knit strips in bright, vibrant colors and patterns. Then sew them together to make a sweater a child will love to wear.

Sizes

To fit 22[24:26:28]in (56[61:66:71]cm) chest.
Length, $14\frac{1}{2}$[16:$17\frac{3}{4}$:$19\frac{1}{4}$]in (36[40:44:48]cm).
Sleeve seam, 10[11:12:13]in (25.5[28:30.5:33.5]cm).

Note: Directions for larger sizes are in brackets [ ]; if there is only one set of figures it applies to all sizes.

Materials

2oz (40g) of a knitting worsted in each of 3 colors, A (green), B (orange) and E (navy)
4oz (80g) in each of 4 colors, C (yellow), D (pale blue), F (red) and G (white)
1 pair each Nos. 3 and 5 ($3\frac{1}{4}$ and 4mm) knitting needles

Gauge

22 sts and 30 rows to 4in (10cm) in stockinette st on No. 5 (4mm) needles.

First strip

Using No. 3 ($3\frac{1}{4}$mm) needles and F, cast on 22[24:26:28] sts. Beg with a K row, work 7 rows stockinette st, then K 1 row to mark hemline.** Change to No. 5 (4mm) needles. Beg with a K row, work 54[60:66:72] rows stockinette st. Change to E and work 2 rows. Beg triangle patt, using separate balls and twisting colors where they join on every row.
***__1st row__ K1 D, K in E to last st, K1 G.
2nd row P1 G, P in E to last st, P1 D.
3rd row As first.
4th row P2 G, P in E to last 2 sts, P2 D.
5th row K2 D, K in E to last 2 sts, K2 G.
6th row P3 G, P in E to last 3 sts, P3 D.
Cont in this way, working 2 sts less in E and one st more into the colors at each side on every 3rd and 2nd row alternately until there are 2 sts left in center in E, ending with a P row. Work 2[2:0:0] rows. 26[28:30:32] rows worked from ***.
Next row K11[12:13:14] D, 11[12:13:14] G.
Next row P11[12:13:14] G, 11[12:13:14] D.
Next row K10[11:12:13] D, 2 E, 10[11:12:13] G.
Cont working patt in reverse, working 2 more sts into E to match first side until 1[1:0:0] sts rem in D and G at each end of row, ending with a P row. Work 0[2:0:2] rows. 52[58:64:70] rows from ***.
****Change to A. K 2 rows. Beg with a K row, work 7 rows stockinette st. Bind off.

Second strip

Work as first strip to **. Change to No. 5

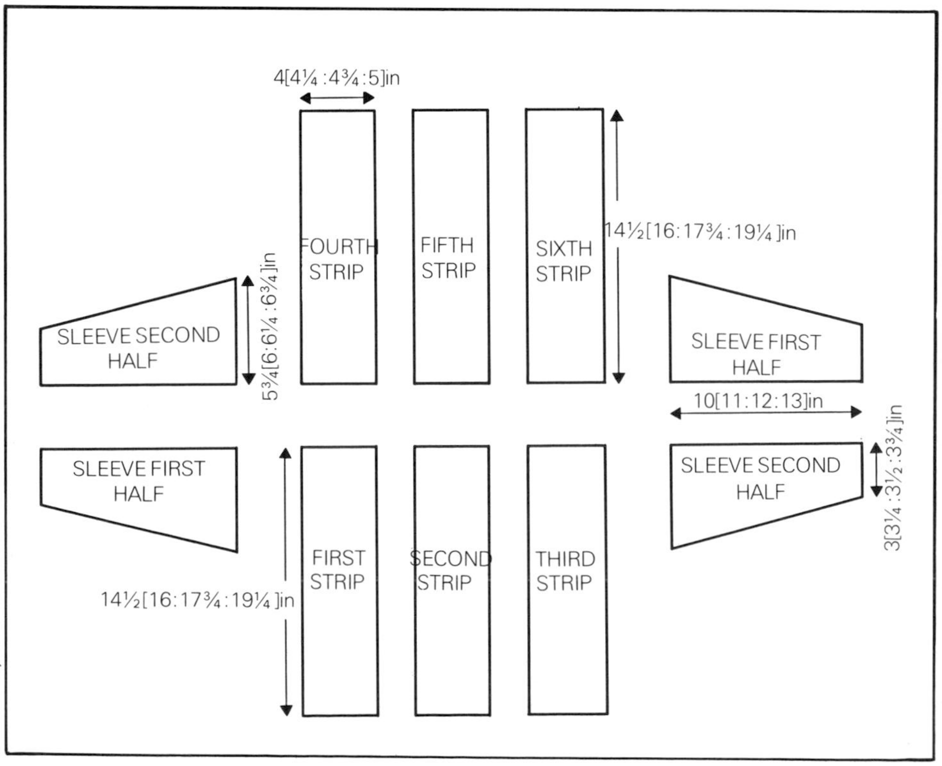
4[4¼:4¾:5]in
FOURTH STRIP
FIFTH STRIP
SIXTH STRIP
14½[16:17¾:19¼]in
5¾[6:6¼:6¾]in
SLEEVE SECOND HALF
SLEEVE FIRST HALF
10[11:12:13]in
SLEEVE FIRST HALF
SLEEVE SECOND HALF
3[3¼:3½:3¾]in
FIRST STRIP
SECOND STRIP
THIRD STRIP
14½[16:17¾:19¼]in
Brian Mayor

(4mm) needles and beg patt.
1st row K7 [8:9:10] G, 8 C, 7 [8:9:10] E.
2nd row P7 [8:9:10] E, 8 C, 7 [8:9:10] G.
Rep these 2 rows 8 [9:10:11] times more.
Next row K7 [8:9:10] G, 15 [16:17:18] C.
Next row P15 [16:17:18] C, 7 [8:9:10] G.
Rep these 2 rows 8 [9:10:11] times more.
Work 18 [20:22:24] rows in G and

54 [60:66:72] rows in A. Using A, work as first strip from **** to end.

Third strip
Work as for first strip to **. Change to No. 5 (4mm) needles. Join in D. Beg with a K row, work 2 rows stockinette st.
3rd row K in D to last st, K1 B.
4th row P1 B, P to end in D.
5th row As 3rd.
6th row P2 B, P to end in D.
7th row K in D to last 2 sts, K2 B.
8th row P3 B, P to end in D.
Cont to work one more st in B and one st less in D on every 3rd and 2nd row alternately until 1 [1:0:0] sts rem in D, ending with a P row. 54 [60:66:72] rows from beg of patt. Cont in stripe sequence of 2 rows each of G, F, G, E, G, D, G, C, G, B, G and A until 54 [60:66:72] rows have been completed; end with a P row. Work as first strip from **** to end.

Fourth strip
Work as first strip to ** but using D instead of F. Change to No. 5 (4mm) needles and work as second strip, but using A instead of G, G instead of C, B instead of E and C instead of A. Work as first strip from **** to end, but using G instead of A.

Fifth strip
Work as first strip to ** but using D instead

of F. Change to No. 5 (4mm) needles and work 54 [60:66:72] rows in stripe patt as at top of third strip. Work as lower part of third strip, but using E instead of D and G instead of B. Work as first strip from **** to end, but using G instead of A.

Sixth strip
Work as first strip to **, but using D instead of F. Change to No. 5 (4mm) needles. Work as first strip using D instead of F, A instead of D, C instead of G and F instead of E. Work as first strip from **** to end, but using G instead of A.

Sleeves
Each sleeve is made in two halves.
First half (make 2)
Using No. 3 (3¼mm) needles and C, cast on 17 [18:19:20] sts. Beg with a K row, work 7 rows stockinette st, then K 1 row to mark hemline. Change to No. 5 (4mm) needles. Beg patt.
1st row K to end in C. **
2nd row P1 D, P to end in C.
3rd row K in C to last st, K1 D.
4th row P2 D, P to end in C.
5th row Using C, inc in first st, K to last 3 sts, K3 D.
6th row P3 D, P to end in C.
Cont as set, working one more st into D on 2 rows, then work 1 row as set, *at the same time* inc at right-hand edge on every 5th row until 34 [38:40:44] rows have been completed. Break off C and D. 23 [25:27:28] sts. Join in F. Work 8 [8:12:12] rows in F, inc as before on every 5th row. Break off F.
Next row K to end in D.
Next row P1 C, P to end in D.
Work one more st into C on next 4 rows, then work 1 row as set. Cont to inc at right-hand edge on every 5th row until there are 31 [33:35:37] sts (still working one more st into C on 5 rows), then one as set, until 76 [84:92:100] rows have been worked from hemline, ending with a P row. Bind off.
Second half (make 2)
Work as first half to **.
2nd row P in C to last st, P1 D.
3rd row K1 D, K to end in C.
Cont to match first half, reversing colors as set and working shaping at left-hand edge.

To finish
Press or block strips according to yarn used.
Join 3 strips for back and 3 for front, matching colors of hems. Turn in hems at top and slip stitch in place. Join shoulder seams, leaving about 8 [8¼:8¾:9] in (20 [21:22:23] cm) open in center for neck. Join two halves of each sleeve. Set in sleeves with center to shoulder seams. Join side and sleeve seams. Turn up hems at lower edge and sleeves and slip stitch in place. Press seams.

Pin patterns

Make these small Victorian heart-shaped pincushions. And then push in pins to form a decorative design.

Belinda

Finished size as desired.

Materials

*Scrap of satin
Scrap of iron-on interfacing
Piece of ¼in (5mm)-wide ribbon to go around pincushion plus a little extra
Suitable stuffing
Silver pins
Paper for pattern
Matching thread*

1 Make a paper pattern of a heart. Cut a piece of paper slightly larger than the size you need.
Fold the paper in half lengthwise.

Draw half a heart, then, keeping the paper folded in half, cut out the heart pattern. Unfold the pattern.
2 Using the pattern, cut out two satin hearts, adding ⅜in (1cm) seam allowance to the edges.
3 From iron-on interfacing cut out two hearts the same size as the fabric hearts.
4 Pin one interfaced heart, shiny side down, on the wrong side of one satin heart, matching the edges. Iron it in place.
5 Repeat step 4 with other heart shapes.
6 Place stiffened hearts together with right sides facing and edges matching. Pin, baste and machine stitch or sew around, taking ⅜in (1cm) seam allowance and leaving a small opening in one side

for turning right side out.
7 Trim seam and turn heart right side out. Stuff firmly. Turn in opening edges; slip stitch them together neatly.
8 Starting at the center top, position the ribbon over the seam, holding it in place with pins placed at ½in (1.3cm) intervals. Bring the ribbon around to the center top, and make a small loop. Cut off excess ribbon; turn under the raw edge and pin it in place.
9 Make a decorative design on one side of the pincushion with pins. Push some pins completely into the cushion and leave some only half-way in for a three-dimensional effect. Glass-headed pins give an interesting effect.

*Making a fabric with
 irregular patchwork shapes
*Pattern for a crazy patchwork
 coat

Making a fabric with irregular patchwork shapes

Patchwork made of separate pieces that are sewn together as the work progresses needs some technical planning beforehand. If possible, use the same type of yarn throughout; if that is impossible, choose yarns of a similar quality and thickness. If you use different stitch patterns, they must all have the same stitch gauge. A simple combination of stockinette stitch, reverse stockinette stitch and variation in the direction of the knitting looks most effective.

In addition to being a perfect medium for blankets, this technique can also be used to make a simple, shaped garment.

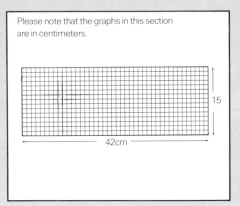

Please note that the graphs in this section are in centimeters.

1 First make a scale drawing of the fabric on graph paper. Here each square represents one square centimeter of fabric. (Centimeters, being smaller than inches, facilitate precise measurements.) Draw the outline of the fabric only (this may include shaping).

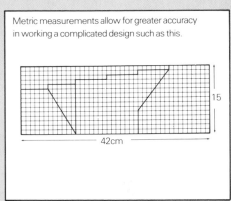

Metric measurements allow for greater accuracy in working a complicated design such as this.

2 Drawing freehand, in pencil initially, divide the fabric into shapes. Keep the shapes reasonably simple, using straight lines and not too many odd angles. When you are satisfied with your arrangement of shapes, use a ruler to join points and straighten the existing freehand lines.

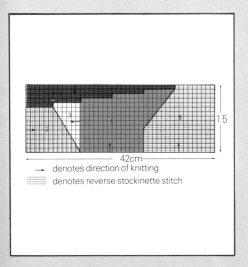

→ denotes direction of knitting
〰 denotes reverse stockinette stitch

3 Complete the scale drawing by numbering and coloring the shapes. This is especially important if you have a large number of shapes and want to make sure that adjacent shapes are in different colors.
Decide on the direction of knitting for each shape; preferably, choose a straight, not diagonal, line as the cast-on edge. Draw in any reverse stockinette stitch texture so that you have a fairly realistic "picture" of the finished fabric.

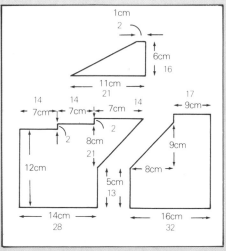

4 Take each shape individually and draw the outline (freehand will do) on plain paper, so that the cast-on edge forms the lower edge on the paper. Count the number of squares on the scale drawing and write in the measurement of each section of the shape (here in black). Calculate the number of stitches and rows to be worked according to the gauge (here in red based on gauge of 19 sts and 26 rows to 10cm).

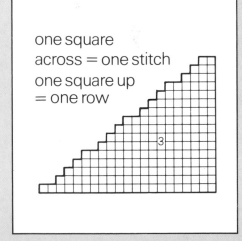

one square
across = one stitch
one square up
= one row

5 Draw each shape again on graph paper (remember that the graph paper will make the shape appear deeper than it will be when knitted). Draw in all the straight lines first, then plan the diagonal lines with either increase and cast-on stitches or decreases and bound-off stitches. If you mix both types of shaping, remember to distribute any cast-on or bound-off stitches evenly to achieve a straight line.

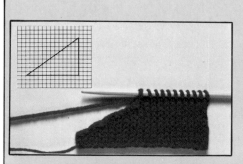 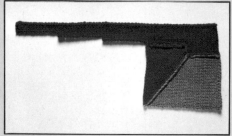 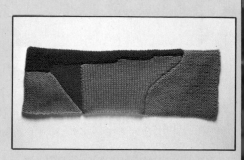

6 The chart forms a visual knitting plan with the precise numbers of stitches, rows and position of shaping clearly marked. The shaping of two lines at different angles may be happening simultaneously, and initially it is easier to keep track of this if you work from a chart. The instructions for the patchwork coat shown here are written out, but if you cannot get used to working from written instructions, you may want to draw your own charts for this pattern.

7 After completing each shape, press or block it and join it into the fabric. Pin the shapes in place first, since you may have to ease some of the shaped edges together. A neat, narrow backstitch seam is the best method of joining.

8 This is the completed fabric on the right side of the work: press or block it according to the type of yarn. The outer edges of the fabric will probably need some type of border to finish them.

Crazy patchwork coat

Choose colors carefully, then make lots of crazy shapes and sew them together to make an elegant patchwork coat. You'll be surprised how easy it is.

Sizes
To fit 32-36in (83-93cm) bust.
Length, 42½in (108cm).
Sleeve seam, 18in (46cm).

Materials
15oz (400g) of a knitting worsted in main shade (A)
15oz (400g) in contrasting color (B)
10oz (250g) in contrasting color (C)
13oz (350g) in contrasting color (D)
1 pair No. 7 (5mm) knitting needles
3 strips leather binding, 1in (3cm) wide and 6¾in (17cm) long
3 buckles

Gauge
19 sts and 26 rows to 4in (10cm) in stockinette st on No. 7 (5mm) needles.

Note:
All shapes are worked on No. 7 (5mm) needles.

Back and fronts
Shape 1 Using A, cast on 17 sts. Beg with a K row, work 2 rows stockinette st. Inc one st at each end of next and every other row until there are 47 sts. P1 row. Dec one st at each end of next and every other row until 17 sts rem. P1 row. Bind off.
Shape 2 Using B, cast on 63 sts.

1st row K to last 2 sts, K2 tog.
2nd row P2 tog, P to end.
3rd row Inc 1, K to last 2 sts, K2 tog.
4th row P2 tog, P to end.
5th row Inc 1, K to last 2 sts, K2 tog.
6th row P2 tog, P to end.
7th row Inc 1, K to last 2 sts, K2 tog.
8th row Bind off 2 sts, P to last st, inc 1. Rep these 8 rows twice more, then first–7th rows again. 44 sts. Dec one st at end of every row until 2 sts rem. Bind off.
Shape 3 Using C, cast on 26 sts. Beg with a P row, cont in reverse stockinette throughout. Dec one st at beg of 3rd and every foll alternate row, *at same time* inc one st at end of 5th and at same edge (left-hand–called LH) on every foll 5th row until 15 inc have been worked at LH edge. Work 3 rows. Bind off.
Shape 4 Using D, cast on 40 sts. Beg with a K row, cont in stockinette st throughout. Dec one st at each end of 5th and every foll 5th row until 10 sts rem. Work 3 rows. Bind off.
Shape 5 Work as given for shape 3, reversing shaping.
Shape 6 Using D, cast on 24 sts. Beg with a K row, cont in stockinette st throughout. Inc one st at end of 3rd and every foll alternate row until there are 39 sts. P1 row. Dec one st at end of next and 2 foll 4th rows, then at end of every

other until 2 sts rem. P1 row. Bind off.
Shape 7 Using B, cast on 37 sts. Beg with a P row, cont in reverse stockinette st throughout. Work 2⅜in (6cm); end with a K row. Inc one st at end of next row and at same edge (LH) on every foll 3rd row until there are 43 sts. P1 row. Cont to inc at LH edge as before, *at same time* dec one st at right-hand (called RH) edge on every row 3 times, then bind off 2 sts at beg of foll row; rep these 4 rows at RH edge until 32 sts rem. Cont to dec at RH edge as before, *at same time* inc one st at LH edge on every row 7 times in all. 31 sts. Bind off.
Shape 8 Using C, cast on 18 sts. Beg with a P row, work 5⅞in (15cm) reverse stockinette st; end with a K row. Bind off.
Shape 9 Using A, cast on 44 sts. Beg with a K row, cont in stockinette st throughout. Dec one st at each end of every row until 28 sts rem. Cont to dec as before at RH edge of shape, dec one st at LH edge on every foll 3rd row until 2 sts rem. K2 tog. Fasten off.
Shape 10 Using B, cast on 18 sts. Beg with a K row, cont in stockinette st throughout. Inc one st at beg of 3rd and every foll alternate row, *at same time* inc one st at beg of 4th and at same edge (LH) on every foll 3rd row until there are 53 sts.
Next row P to end.

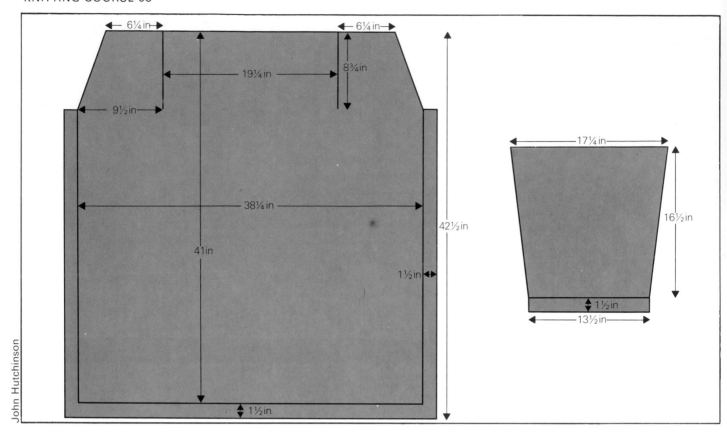

John Hutchinson

Next row K2 tog, K to end.
Next row Inc 1, P to end.
Next row K2 tog, K to end.
Cont to dec one st at beg of alternate rows at RH edge, *at same time* bind off 2 sts, then dec one st alternately at beg of rows at LH edge until 2 sts rem. K2 tog. Fasten off.
Shape 11 Using C, cast on 27 sts. Beg with a P row, cont in reverse stockinette st throughout. Dec one st at beg of 4th row and at same edge (LH) on every foll 3rd row, *at same time* dec one st at RH edge on 6th and every foll 5th row until 2 sts rem.
Next row K2.
Next row P2 tog. Fasten off.
Shape 12 Using D, cast on 44 sts. Beg with a K row, work 2 rows stockinette st. Inc one st at beg of next and every foll 4th row, *at same time* dec one st at end of next row and at same edge (LH) on next, then foll alternate row; rep last 3 rows of sequence until 7th inc has been worked at RH edge; end with a K row. P 1 row. Cont to inc at RH edge as before, inc one st at LH edge on next 4 rows, then foll alternate row; rep last 4 rows of sequence until there are 51 sts; end with a P row. Cont to inc at LH edge as before, bind off 3 sts at beg of next row. Dec one st at end (RH) edge of next row, bind off 2 sts at beg of foll row, dec one st at end of next row and bind off 3 sts at beg of foll row; rep this 4-row sequence until 34 sts rem; end with a K row. Inc one st at beg and dec one st at end of next row. Bind off.

Shape 13 Using B, cast on 44 sts. P 1 row. Cont in reverse stockinette st throughout, dec one st at beg of next row and at same edge (LH) on foll row. Dec one st at LH edge on next 2 rows, then on foll alternate row; rep this 4-row sequence, *at same time* inc one st at RH edge on 6th and every foll 7th row until 23 sts rem; end with a P row.
Next row K2 tog, K to last st, inc 1.
Next row Bind off 4, P to last 2 sts, P2 tog.
Next row Bind off 2, K to last 2 sts, K2 tog.
Next row Bind off 5, P to last 2 sts, P2 tog.
Next row Bind off 2, K to last 2 sts, K2 tog.
Bind off rem 6 sts.
Shape 14 Using A, cast on 31 sts. Beg with a K row, cont in stockinette st, dec one st at end of 4th and at same edge (RH) on every foll 3rd row until 18 sts rem; end with a K row.
Next row P2 tog, P to end.
Next row K2 tog, K to end.
Next row P to end.
Keeping RH edge straight, cont to dec at LH edge over next 7 rows (dec one st on first, 2nd, 5th and 6th rows); rep this sequence until 5 sts rem; end with a P row. Cont to dec at LH edge as before, *at same time* inc one st at RH edge on next, then every 3rd and alternate row alternately until 2 sts rem. Fasten off.
Shape 15 Using A, cast on 74 sts. P 1 row. Cont in reverse stockinette st throughout, dec one st at RH edge on 3rd, then 3 foll alternate rows; rep this

sequence, *at same time* dec one st at LH edge on every 3rd row until 49 sts rem; end with a K row. Cont to dec at LH edge as before, dec one st at RH edge on every row until 40 sts rem; end with a P row. Dec one st at RH edge on next, then every 3rd and 4th row alternately, *at same time* at LH edge bind off 3 sts at beg of next row, then dec one st at same edge of foll 3 rows; rep this sequence until one st rem. Fasten off.
Shape 16 Using C, cast on 25 sts. Beg with a K row, cont in stockinette st until work measures 7⅞in (20cm); end with a K row. Keeping RH edge straight, dec one st at LH edge on next 2 rows. Bind off 2 sts at beg of next row and dec one st at same edge on foll row; rep this sequence until 3 sts rem. P3 tog. Fasten off.
Shape 17 Using D, cast on 59 sts. Beg with a P row, cont in reverse stockinette st until work measures 10⅝in (27cm); end with a P row. Dec one st at each end of next 7 rows; end with a K row.
Next row Bind off 2 sts, work to last 2 sts, work 2 tog.
Rep last row until 18 sts rem; end with a P row. Bind off.
Shape 18 Using B, cast on 67 sts. Beg with a K row, work 3½in (9cm) stockinette st; end with a P row. Bind off.
Shape 19 Using D, cast on 67 sts. P 1 row. Cont in reverse stockinette st throughout, dec one st at beg of next row and at same edge (LH) on every row until 2 sts rem. P2 tog. Fasten off.
Shape 20 Using A, cast on 82 sts. K 1 row. Cont in stockinette st throughout,

dec one st at end of next row and at same edge (RH) on every row until 57 sts rem; end with a P row. Cont to dec at RH edge as before, dec one st at LH edge on next and every foll 5th row until 39 sts rem; end with a K row.

Cont to dec at LH edge as before, dec one st at RH edge on alternate rows until 34 sts rem; end with a P row. Dec one st at beg of every row until 17 sts rem; end with a K row.

Next row Bind off 4, P to end.
Next row K2 tog, K to last 2 sts, K2 tog.
Next row Bind off 4, P to end.
Next row K to last 2 sts, K2 tog. Bind off rem 6 sts.

Shape 21 Using B, cast on 52 sts. Beg with a P row, work 1½in (4cm) reverse stockinette st; end with a P row. Inc one st at end (RH edge) of next and 3 foll 4th rows. 56 sts. P 1 row. Inc one st at RH edge on next 2 rows. Cast on 2 sts at end (RH edge) of next row and inc one st at same edge on foll 3 rows; rep this 4-row sequence until there are 75 sts; end with a K row. P 1 row. *Dec one st at end of next row. Bind off 4 sts at beg (RH edge)

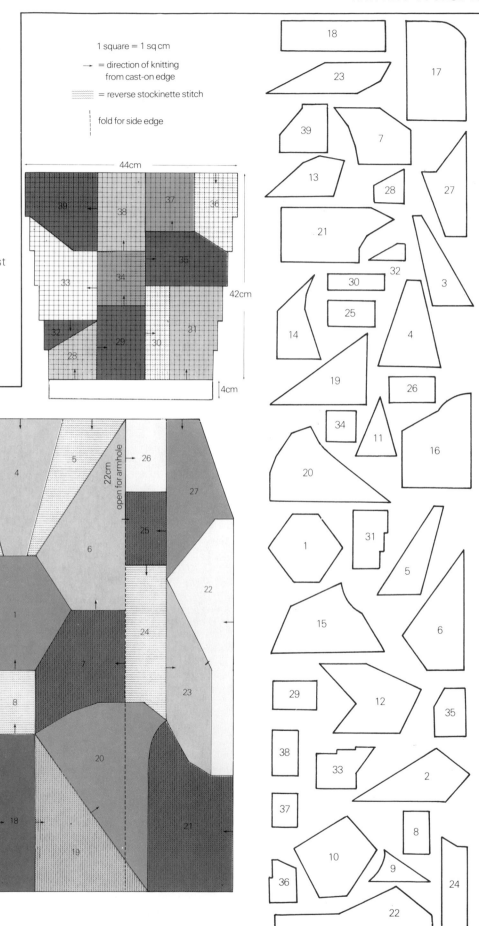

John Hutchinson

of next row and dec one st at same edge on foll 2 rows; rep from * until 53 sts rem; end with a K row. Bind off.

Shape 22 Using C, cast on 105 sts. Beg with a K row, work 1½in (4cm) stockinette st; end with a P row. Dec one st at beg of next row. Work 1 row, then dec 1 st at same edge (RH) on foll 4 rows; rep this 5-row sequence, *at same time* when work measures 2in (5cm); end with a K row, cont as foll:
Next row Bind off 44, patt to end.
Cont to dec at RH edge as before, dec one st at LH edge on next row and bind off 2 sts at the same edge on foll row; rep this sequence until 3 sts rem. K 3 tog. Fasten off.

Shape 23 Using D, cast on 57 sts.
1st row K to end.
2nd row P2 tog, P to last st, inc 1.
3rd row Inc 1, K to last 2 sts, K2 tog.
4th row Bind off 2, P to last st, inc 1.
5th row Cast on 2 sts, K to last 2 sts, K2 tog.
6th row As 4th.
Rep 3rd–6th rows twice more, then 3rd–5th rows again. Cont to dec at LH edge as before, inc one st at RH edge on every other row until 44 sts rem; end with a K row. Bind off.

Shape 24 Using C, cast on 17 sts. Beg with a P row, work 11⅜in (29cm) reverse stockinette st; end with a K row. Bind off 8 sts at beg (RH edge) of next row. Dec one st at RH edge on next 3 rows and foll alternate row; rep this sequence until 2 sts rem. K2 tog. Fasten off.

Shape 25 Using B, cast on 31 sts. Beg with a P row, work 3½in (9cm) reverse stockinette st; end with a K row. Bind off.

Shape 26 As shape 25, but work in C and stockinette st.

Shape 27 Using A, cast on 14 sts. Beg

with a K row, cont in stockinette st, inc one st at beg of 4th row and at same edge (LH) on every foll 4th, then 3rd row alternately until there are 29 sts; end with a K row. Work 4 rows stockinette st, then bind off 8 sts at beg of foll row. Keeping RH edge straight, dec one st at LH edge at end of 3rd row. Cont to dec at LH edge on next, then foll alternate row; rep this 3-row sequence until 2 sts rem. Work 2 rows. K2 tog. Fasten off.

Sleeves (alike)
Shape 28 Using D, cast on 20 sts. Beg with a P row, work 2⅜in (6cm) reverse stockinette st, end with a P row.
**Bind off 2 sts at beg of next row, then dec one st at same edge (LH) on next 3 rows; rep this sequence until 2 sts rem.
**. K2 tog. Fasten off.

Shape 29 Using B, cast on 30 sts. Beg with a K row, work 4in (10cm) stockinette st; end with a P row. Bind off.

Shape 30 Using C, cast on 36 sts. Beg with a P row, work 2in (5cm) reverse stockinette st; end with a K row. Bind off.

Shape 31 Using D, cast on 17 sts. Beg with a K row, work 2⅜in (6cm) stockinette st; end with a P row. Cast on 2 sts at beg of next row, then work a further 2⅜in (6cm) stockinette st; end with a P row. Cast on 2 sts at beg of next row, then cont straight until work measures 7½in (19cm); end with a P row. Bind off.

Shape 32 Using B, cast on 21 sts. K 1 row. Cont in stockinette st, work as shape 28 from ** to **. Bind off.

Shape 33 Using C, cast on 28 sts. Beg with a K row, work 2in (5cm) stockinette st; end with a P row. Inc one st at beg of next row and at same edge (RH) on next and foll alternate row; rep this 3-row sequence until there are 40 sts; end with

a K row.
Next row Bind off 14, P to end.
Next row Inc 1, K to end.
Next row Bind off 14, P to last st, inc 1.
Next row K to end.
Bind off rem 14 sts.

Shape 34 Using A, cast on 20 sts. Beg with a P row, work 4¼in (11cm) reverse stockinette st; end with a K row. Bind off.

Shape 35 Using B, cast on 21 sts. Beg with a K row, work 4in (10cm) stockinette st; end with a P row. Dec one st at end of next row and at same edge (LH) on foll 3rd, then 2nd rows alternately until 14 sts rem. Work 2 rows. Bind off.

Shape 36 Using C, cast on 17 sts. Beg with a P row, work 3½in (9cm) reverse stockinette st; end with a P row. Bind off 2 sts at beg of next row, then cont in reverse stockinette st until work measures 4¾in (12cm); end with a P row. Dec one st at end of next row and at same edge (RH) on foll 2 rows, then bind off 2 sts at beg of next row; rep this 4-row sequence twice more.

Shape 37 Using A, cast on 20 sts. Beg with a K row, work 4¾in (12cm) stockinette st; end with a P row. Bind off.

Shape 38 Using D, cast on 20 sts. Beg with a K row, work 5⅞in (15cm) stockinette st; end with a P row. Bind off.

Shape 39 Using B, cast on 32 sts. Beg with a P row, work 2in (5cm) reverse stockinette st; end with a P row. Dec one st at beg of next row and at same edge (LH) on foll 2 alternate rows; rep this 5-row sequence until 17 sts rem. Work 1 row. Bind off.

Collar
Using No. 7 (5mm) needles and B, cast on 32 sts for back neck. Cont in garter st throughout, work 2 rows. Cast on 5 sts at beg of next 6 rows. 62 sts. Cont straight until collar measures 4¾in (12cm) at center back. Bind off.

To finish
Press or block shapes according to yarn used. Using a fine backstitch seam, join shapes into fabric for back, fronts and sleeves as shown in diagram, leaving 8⅝in (22cm) open in side seams for armholes. Join shoulder seams. Sew on collar with shaped edges coming about 3⅛in (8cm) down front neck edge.
Lower border Using No. 7 (5mm) needles and A, cast on 8 sts. Cont in garter st until border fits along entire lower edge. Bind off. Sew border in place. Make a similar border for lower edge of sleeves and sew in place. Join sleeve seams. Set in sleeves.
Front border Work as for lower border until border fits entire front edge as far up as collar, then along short edge of collar. Sew in place, reversing seam along edge of collar. Use leather binding and buckles to make fastenings as shown in photograph.

Knitting / COURSE 69

*Working patchwork
 texture in separate pieces
*Working patchwork
 texture within a fabric
*Pattern for a patchwork
 sweater

Working patchwork texture in separate pieces

The previous courses on patchwork knitting concentrated mainly on shape and color. However, many interesting patchworks can be made with different types of textured yarn including bouclé, tweed, mohair and glitter.

Combine yarn textures with those created by stitch patterns and you have a "landscaped" fabric of shape and texture. A subtle use of color—such as tones of one color—emphasizes the design.

This type of patchwork is perfect for experimenting with yarn and for working out your own designs. Often the yarn and textures may be so interesting that you need only use square or rectangular shapes for maximum effect.

All the yarns must be approximately the same in weight. Each shape is worked separately, since the different varieties of yarn and stitch patterns each produce their own gauge. It is impossible to make a successful one-piece fabric with various types of yarn unless they are all *exactly* the same gauge.

Assemble a variety of yarns that you want to use in the patchwork: some yarns may be left over from other garments. It is particularly important that all the yarns be similar in weight and can be either hand-washed or dry-cleaned. Choose the colors carefully: here they are all tones of one color.

The easiest patchwork texture is a regular fabric with rectangular patches. Cast on varying numbers of stitches for each patch (so that they are different widths), but knit each patch to the same depth in any stitch pattern you choose. Here the depth is the unifying factor and it is not necessary, in this case, for the stitch gauges to tally.

continued

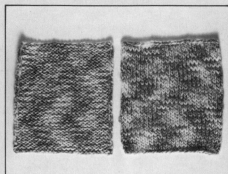

1 Before beginning to knit, experiment with different yarns and stitch patterns. Some yarns do not enhance certain patterns and vice versa. Here you can see the clearly defined texture of seed stitch worked in ordinary yarn against a similar patch in mohair where all definition has been lost.

2 With textured patchwork, always consider whether you are showing a yarn or stitch pattern to its best advantage. The reverse stockinette stitch sample in tweed yarn here shows how the texture of the stitch adds to the character of the yarn. The same yarn worked in smooth stockinette stitch shows the various colors against a flat background.

3 To construct a finished fabric, sew the patches together in strips matching the depth. You can make the depth of each strip the same throughout or vary the depth of the strips.

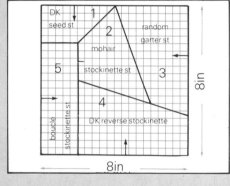

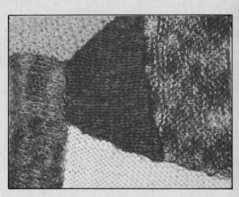

4 You can also make a textured patchwork with irregular shapes, but this is quite difficult. First make a scale drawing of the completed fabric; indicate the direction of the knitting with an arrow and code each shape so that you have a master plan to work from (see page 41).

5 Make a gauge sample for each type of yarn and stitch pattern that you are using. According to the gauge, plan each shape stitch by stitch and row by row on graph paper—again, see page 41. Here are the first three shapes from the plan in step 4.

6 Using a narrow backstitch seam, join the shapes together after each one is complete to ensure a good fit. Note that in the finished fabric here the stitches and directions of the knitting may vary from patch to patch: this is an important factor when you are designing the fabric.

There are innumerable combinations of yarn and stitch textures; here are just three of them.
In this fabric the yarn texture and coloring are the main features. Each shape is worked in stockinette stitch with different types of yarn.

This fabric is a collection of various stitch patterns. Their individual textures are so interesting that they look best in ordinary knitting worsted yarn: in this way the yarn does not detract from the patterns.

A very effective fabric can be made from different qualities of knitting worsted yarn such as plain, multi-colored and random-dyed. Combine them with simple stitch patterns to enhance the qualities of the yarn.

Working patchwork texture within a fabric

It is possible to employ jacquard knitting techniques (using a small, separate ball of yarn for each shape) to create a patchwork texture without sewing together separately worked patches.

The best results are obtained by using one quality of yarn, such as knitting worsted, in a number of variations including tweed, multi-colored and random-dyed; in this way the stitch gauge of each yarn is the same and they can be safely knitted into one fabric.

As stitch patterns have varying gauges, work throughout in stockinette stitch and reverse stockinette stitch; this simple combination creates an effective contrast of textures.

Irregular shapes within the fabric create more interest in the textures. Since you are knitting an entire fabric, the stitches lie in one direction. When working separate patches, vary the direction.

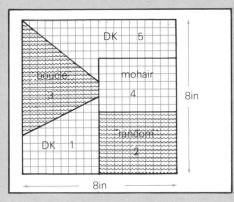

1 Collect a range of different types of yarn, having first checked that they all have the same stitch gauge on the needles you are using.
Make a scale drawing of the fabric, mark the shapes, and decide on the yarn and stitch for each shape.

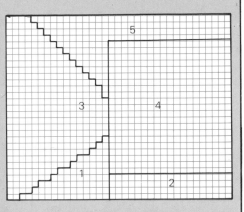

2 Make a chart of the entire fabric on graph paper. The center section of the design shown here is based on a gauge of 22 stitches and 30 rows to 4in (10cm). The straight horizontal and vertical lines are easy to locate, but diagonal lines may take some time to work out.

3 Using the chart as a pattern, cast on the entire number of stitches—44— across the lower edge of the fabric, using a separate ball of yarn for each shape. The fabric is knitted jacquard-style throughout with a separate ball of yarn for each shape, twisting the yarns at the change-over to prevent a hole.

4 Although several balls of yarn have been used simultaneously to produce this fabric, it is a single thickness. Here you can see the techniques involved on the wrong side of the work.

5 Here is the complete fabric from the right side. A patchwork fabric has been created without having to sew many shapes together. If the various stitch gauges correspond exactly, the work lies flat; otherwise it is pulled out of shape by the different gauges.

Fred Mancini

Patchwork sweater

Follow our detailed charts and make this stunning patchwork sweater. It's knitted in a range of matching solid- and multi-colored yarns. The possible combinations of color and texture are almost endless.

Sizes
To fit 32[34:36]in (83[87:92]cm) bust.
Length, 23½in (60cm).
Sleeve seam, 19in (48cm).

Note: Directions for larger sizes are in brackets []; if there is only one set of figures it applies to all sizes.

Materials
A knitting worsted-weight yarn 8[8:10]oz (200[200:250]g) in color(A) 4[4:6]oz (100[100:150]g) each in colors (B and C) 4oz (100g) in color (D); 1 pair each Nos. 3 and 6 (3¼ and 4½mm) knitting needles

Gauge
22 sts to 4in (10cm) on No. 6 (4½mm) needles.

Front
**Using No. 3 (3¼mm) needles and A, cast on 96[102:108]sts.
1st ribbing row P1[2:1], K2, *P2, K2, rep

from * to last 1[2:1] sts, P1[2:1].
2nd ribbing row K1[2:1], P2, *K2, P2, rep from * to last 1[2:1] sts, K1[2:1].
Rep these 2 rows for 3¼in (8cm); end with a 2nd ribbing row. **Change to No. 6 (4½mm) needles. Beg with a K row, work 8[8:6] rows stockinette st. Reading RS rows from right to left and WS rows from left to right and twisting yarns when changing color to prevent a hole, starting at 9th[9th:7th] row of chart 1 (see page 51), cont working from chart in color and st as stated. Work until 142nd row has been worked, then dec at neck edge and bind off sts for shoulder as indicated.

Back

Work as front from ** to **. Change to No. 6 (4½mm) needles. Reading RS rows from right to left and WS rows from left to right and twisting yarns when changing color to prevent a hole, cont working from chart 2 (see page 52) in color and st as stated. Work until 154th row has been worked, then dec at neck edge and bind off sts for shoulder as indicated.

Right sleeve

With No. 3 (3¼mm) needles and A, cast on 46 sts.
1st ribbing row *P2, K2, rep from * to last 2 sts, P2.
2nd ribbing row *K2, P2, rep from * to last 2 sts, K2.
Rep these 2 rows for 3¼in (8cm); end with a 2nd ribbing row. Change to No. 6 (4½mm) needles and cont working from chart 3 (see page 53) in st and color stated on chart **and at same time** inc one st at each end of 5th and every foll 6th row until there are 80[82:82] sts. Work 19[13:13] rows straight. Bind off loosely.

Left sleeve

As right sleeve, but work from chart 4 (see page 53).

Neckband

Join right shoulder seam. With RS facing join A to left front neck and using No. 3 (3¼mm) needles pick up and K 21 sts along left side neck, K sts from holder, pick up and K 21 sts along right front neck, 5 sts down right back neck, K sts from holder inc 4 sts evenly, then pick up and K 5 sts up left back neck. 90 sts.
1st ribbing row *K2, P2, rep from * to last 2 sts, K2.
2nd ribbing row *P2, K2, rep from * to last 2 sts, P2.
Rep these 2 rows 3 times more. Bind off loosely in ribbing.

To finish

Block or press. Join left shoulder seam. Mark depth of armholes 7[7¼:7¼]in (18[18.5:18.5]cm) from shoulder seams on back and front, sew sleeves to armholes between markers. Join side and sleeve seams.

Rod Delroy

CHART 1

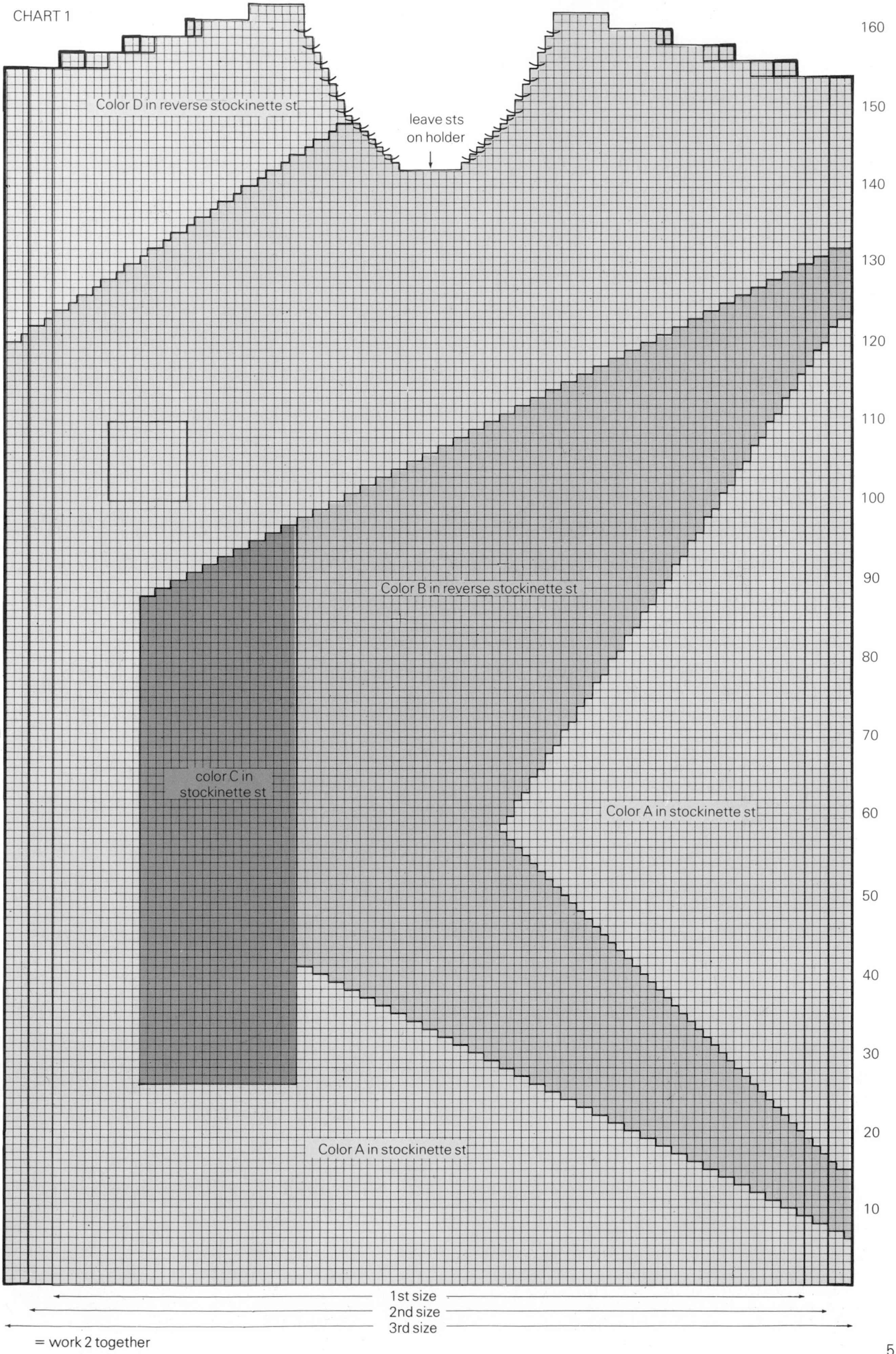

160

Color D in reverse stockinette st

150

leave sts
on holder
↓

140

130

120

Color B in reverse stockinette st

110

100

90

Color A in stockinette st

80

70

color C in
stockinette st

60

50

Color A in stockinette st

40

30

20

Color A in stockinette st

10

John Hutchinson

1st size

2nd size

3rd size

= work 2 together

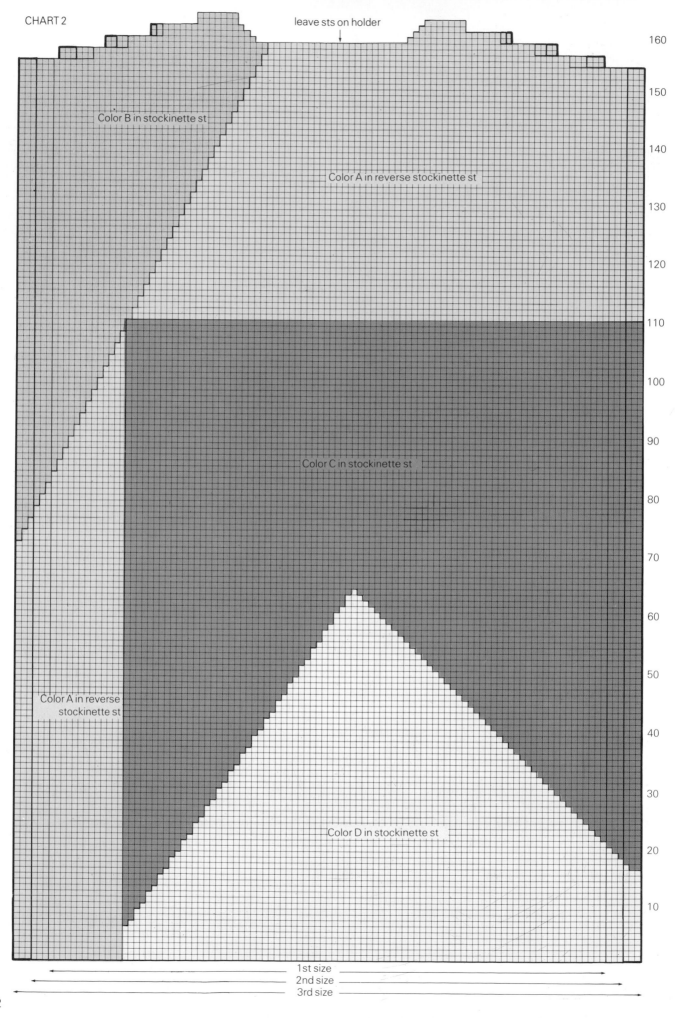

CHART 2

leave sts on holder

Color B in stockinette st

Color A in reverse stockinette st

Color C in stockinette st

Color A in reverse
stockinette st

Color D in stockinette st

160

150

140

130

120

110

100

90

80

70

60

50

40

30

20

10

1st size
2nd size
3rd size

52

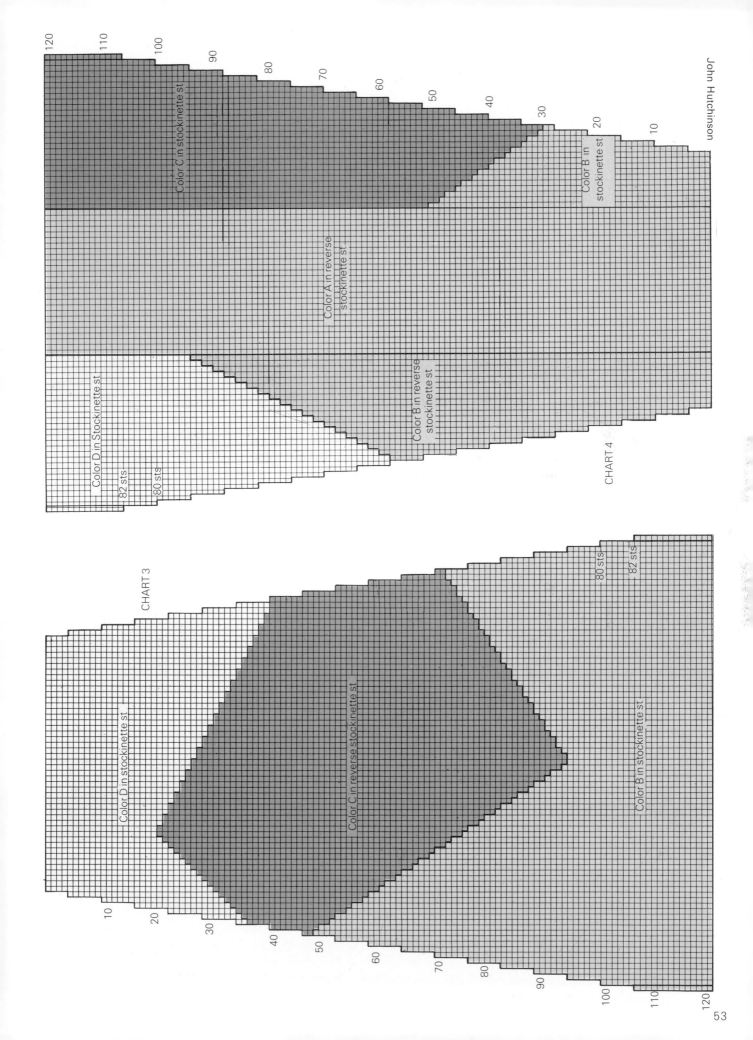

CHART 4

Color C in stockinette st

Color B in stockinette st

Color A in reverse stockinette st

Color B in reverse stockinette st

Color D in Stockinette st

82 sts

80 sts

CHART 3

Color D in stockinette st

Color C in reverse stockinette st

Color B in stockinette st

80 sts

82 sts

Wooly people

These little people, made from bits of yarn and embroidery thread, are ideal "doll house" dolls. They can also be hung together to make a simple mobile.

Materials
Bits of yarn in different colors
Bits of embroidery thread in different colors
Matching sewing thread

1 Start by winding the yarn around the flattened palm of your hand. Keep on winding the yarn to form a band 1in (2.5cm) thick. Cut off yarn.

2 Remove the skein from your hand. Wind a short length of yarn tightly around the skein about ¾in (2cm) from one end for the doll's head. Tie off the yarn and thread the end into the skein.

3 Tie the skein again about 1in (2.5cm) below the first knot to form the body.

4 Divide the rest of the skein into two equal thicknesses for the legs. Tie each end of the leg about ½in (1.3cm) from the end for the feet.

5 For the arms, wind some more yarn around three fingers to form a band the same thickness as the legs; cut off yarn. Remove the skein and tie it ½in (1.3cm) from each end for hands.

6 Thread the arms through the center of the doll's body so that there is an equal amount on each side. Sew the arms to the body with matching thread.

7 Embroider the eyes and mouth on the doll's face using embroidery thread in different colors.

8 To hang the doll up, use a length of matching yarn; thread it through the top of the head and knot.

9 To make larger dolls, wind the yarn around a piece of cardboard the desired size.

Knitting / COURSE 70

*Knitting in rounds to make gloves
*Stitch Wise: Italian and French patterns
*Patterns for man's and woman's hat, scarf and glove sets

Knitting in rounds to make gloves

Gloves are traditionally knitted in rounds on a set of four needles: the obvious advantage of this is the absence of seams on a small item where they would be superfluous and uncomfortable, although it is possible to make gloves in flat knitting.

As making gloves is somewhat complex, first practice knitting in rounds as shown in Volume 6, pages 45 and 46. It is especially important to mark the beginning of rounds; otherwise your shaping for right and left gloves is likely to be confused.

The step-by-step illustrations here are based on the instructions for the man's right glove on page 59, but the same techniques can be used on most knitted gloves.

1 The shaping for the thumb starts in the main pattern section (stockinette stitch in this case) after the ribbed cuff. Here the 4th round (first increase round) has just been worked: 2 stitches—one at each side of the gusset—are increased by picking up the loop lying between stitches and knitting it through the back.

2 The thumb gusset is marked at each side by a purl stitch. As the 2 stitches are increased within the gusset on every 3rd round it becomes a triangular shape. The thumb shaping is complete when there are 17 stitches between the purl "markers" (14 stitches increased).

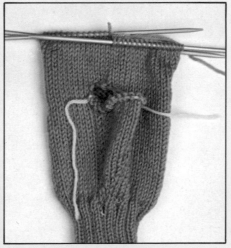

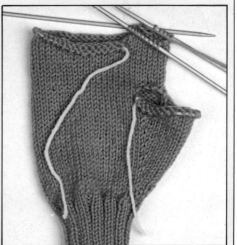

3 Work 5 rounds in stockinette stitch. On the next round, separate the thumb stitches from the rest of the hand and leave them until later—"K1, sl next 17 sts onto a thread for thumb, turn work and cast on 3 sts, K to end. 48 sts."

4 There are now the original number of stitches on the needles. Continue in rounds of stockinette stitch for 1½in (4cm) without shaping to form the section of the hand between thumb joint and start of fingers. Remember to finish knitting at the end of a round.

5 Start working the first finger—"K7, turn and cast on 2 sts (to give three-dimensional depth to the finger), sl next 34 sts onto a thread (there is no need to fasten this length of contrasting-colored yarn, which should be long enough to hang free at each end), K rem 7 sts (using a third needle)."

continued

Mike Berend

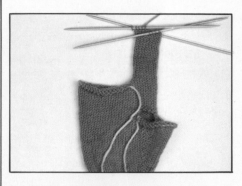

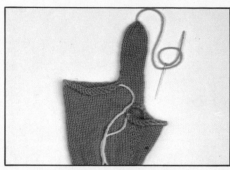

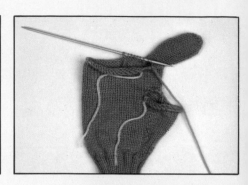

6 Divide the 16 stitches for the first finger between three needles. Continue in rounds of stockinette stitch for length of finger: each finger has a different length—here it is 6¼in (16cm) for a man's hand (women's fingers are generally ¼in [5mm] shorter).

7 The top of the finger has 2 rounds of shaping—knit 2 stitches together, then knit 1 stitch alternately on the first round, then knit 2 stitches together across the second round. Cut off the yarn, leaving a long end. Thread the end through the remaining stitches, pull together and fasten off.

8 Pick up stitches from the thread for the second finger. With the back of the hand facing you, slip the last 7 stitches on the thread onto a needle; withdraw the thread. Rejoin the yarn to the last stitch on the needle; pick up and knit 2 stitches from the 2 cast-on stitches at the base of the first finger.

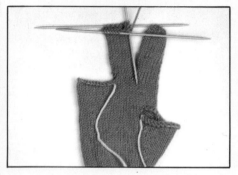

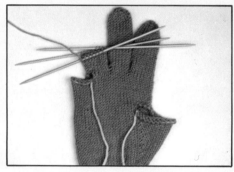

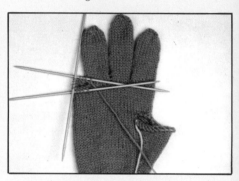

9 Slip the last 5 stitches at the palm end of the thread onto another needle, then knit across them. Turn the work and cast on 2 stitches. Divide these 16 stitches between three needles—the shorter the needles the better for this small number of stitches. Work to match first finger, making this finger 3¼in (8cm) in length.

10 Following steps 8 and 9, collect 16 stitches for the third finger—from the thread at the back, from the base of the second finger, from the thread across the palm—and cast on 2 stitches. Again work to match the first finger, making this finger the same length.

11 There are now 10 stitches remaining on the thread for the fourth finger. Knit across these stitches, then pick up and knit 2 stitches from base of third finger. Divide the 12 stitches between 3 needles: make this "little" finger 2¼in (6cm) in length. Shape top by simply knitting 2 stitches together across last round.

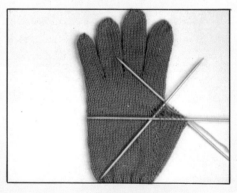

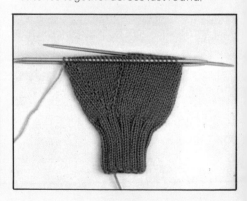

12 Return to the 17 thumb stitches on the thread and slip them onto a needle, then pick up and knit 3 stitches from those cast on at the base of the thumb. Work in rounds of stockinette stitch for 2¼in (6cm). The top of the thumb has an extra round where a plain round is worked between the 2 shaping rounds used for the top of the main fingers.

13 The finished glove needs no assembling, except that the ends of yarn at the ends of the fingers and thumb must be darned in. The thumb gusset shaping determines the position of the thumb: here it "sits" on the palm of the glove.

14 The left glove is made in exactly the same way as the right, but the position of the thumb gusset is reversed. On the right glove the gusset shaping is at the beginning of a round; on the left glove it must be at the end of a round. Here is the gusset shaping completed on the left glove.

Stitch Wise

Italian brocade pattern

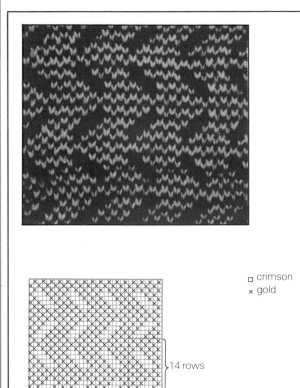

□ crimson
× gold

14 rows

repeat 8 sts

Italian tulip border

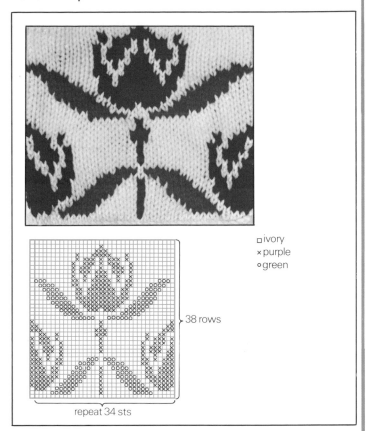

□ ivory
× purple
○ green

38 rows

repeat 34 sts

French woven pattern

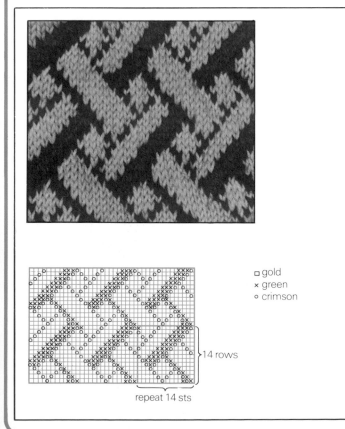

□ gold
× green
○ crimson

14 rows

repeat 14 sts

French checked jacquard

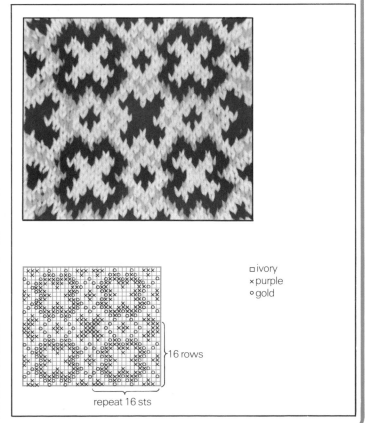

□ ivory
× purple
○ gold

16 rows

repeat 16 sts

Mike Berend

Brian Mayor

Man's and woman's hat, scarf and glove sets

These knitted accessories will keep out chilly winter winds.

Man's set

Sizes
Hat to fit average man's head.
Scarf, 67in (170cm) long.
Gloves around hand, 8in (20cm). Length, 10¼in (26cm).

Materials
Hat *4oz (80g) of a sport yarn in main color (A)*
2oz (40g) in each of 3 contrasting colors (B, C and D)
Scarf *8oz (200g) in (A)*
2oz (40g) in each of (B, C and D)
Gloves *2oz (40g) in each of (A, B, C and D)*
Complete set *11oz (280g) in (A)*
2oz (40g) in each of (B, C and D)
1 pair No. 6 (4½mm) knitting needles
Set of four Nos. 3, 5 and 6 (3¼, 4 and 4½mm) double-pointed needles

Gauge
22 sts and 30 rows to 4in (10cm) in stockinette st on No. 6 (4½mm) needles.
24 sts and 32 rows to 4in (10cm) in stockinette st on No. 5 (4mm) needles.

Hat
Using set of four No. 6 (4½mm) needles and A, cast on 112 sts. Work in rounds of K2, P2 ribbing for 6¼in (16cm). Change to No. 5 (4mm) needles and work a further 1½in (4cm) ribbing. Change to No. 6 (4½mm) needles. Cont in rounds of stockinette st (every round K) and stripe sequence of 4 rows B and 2 rows each of D, C, A, C and D throughout, until work measures 4in (10cm) from beg of stockinette st.

Shape top
1st round *K12, K2 tog, rep from * to end.
2nd and every alternate round K to end.
3rd round *K11, K2 tog, rep from * to end.
Cont to dec in this way on every alternate round until 16 sts rem. K 1 round.
Next round K2 tog to end.
Cut off yarn, thread through sts, pull to gather and fasten off.

Scarf

Using No. 6 (4½mm) needles and A, cast on 70 sts. Work 4in (10cm) K2, P2 ribbing. Cont in ribbing, work 4 rows B, 2 rows each of D, C, A, C, D and 4 rows B. Cont in A only until work measures 60in (152cm). Work 18 rows stripe sequence as before. Cont in A only for 4in (10cm). Bind off in ribbing.

Fringe Cut yarn into 14in (35cm) lengths, then, taking one strand from each color together, knot into every K rib along each end. Trim fringe.

Right glove

Using set of four No. 3 (3¼mm) needles and A, cast on 48 sts. Work in rounds of K2, P2 ribbing for 2¼in (6cm). Change to No. 5 (4mm) needles. Cont in rounds of stockinette st (every round K) and stripe sequence as for hat, shape as foll:

1st round P1, K3, P1, K to end.
2nd and 3rd rounds As first.
4th round P1, K1, pick up loop lying between needles and K tbl—called make 1 (M1)—, K1, M1, K1, P1, K to end.
5th and 6th rounds P1, K5, P1, K to end.
7th round P1, K1, M1, K3, M1, K1, P1, K to end.
Cont to inc in this way on every 3rd round until there are 62 sts. Work 5 rounds.
***Next round** K1, sl next 17 sts onto a thread for thumb, turn and cast on 3 sts, K to end. 48 sts.
Work 1½in (4cm) in rounds of stockinette st. Cut off 3 contrasting colors and cont with A only.

First finger

K7, turn and cast on 2 sts, sl next 34 sts onto a thread, K rem 7 sts. Work 2¾in (7cm) on these 16 sts.

Shape top

Next round *K1, K2 tog, rep from * to last st, K1.
Next round K2 tog to last st, K1.
Cut off yarn, thread through sts, pull to gather and fasten off.

Second finger

K 7 sts from back of hand, pick up and K 2 sts from base of first finger, K5 sts from palm, turn and cast on 2 sts. 16 sts. Complete as for first finger, making length 3¼in (8cm) instead of 2¾in (7cm).

Third finger

Pick up sts as for second finger, then work as for first finger, making length the same.

Fourth finger

K rem 10 sts, pick up and K 2 sts from base of third finger. 12 sts. Work 2¼in (6cm) stockinette st.

Shape top

Next round K2 tog to end.
Cut off yarn, thread through sts, pull to gather and fasten off.

Thumb

Sl 17 sts from thread onto needles, pick up and K3 sts from cast-on sts at base of thumb. Work 2¼in (6cm) in A on these 20 sts.

Shape top

Next round K2 tog, *K1, K2 tog, rep from * to end.
Next round K to end.
Next round K1, (K2 tog) to end.
Cut off yarn, thread through sts, pull to gather and fasten off.

Left glove

Work as for right glove, reversing shaping after ribbing as foll:
1st round K to last 5 stitches, P1, K3, P1.
2nd and 3rd rounds As first.
4th round K to last 5 sts, P1, K1, M1, K1, M1, K1, P1.

Woman's set

Sizes: Hat to fit average head.
Scarf, 67in (170cm) long.
Gloves around hand, 7in (18cm).
Length, 9½in (24cm).

Materials

Hat *4oz (80g) of a random-dyed sport yarn*
Scarf *8oz (200g)*
Gloves *4oz (80g)*
Complete set *12oz (320g)*
1 pair No. 6 (4½mm) knitting needles
Set of four Nos. 3, 5 and 6 (3¼, 4 and 4½mm) double-pointed needles

Gauge

22 sts and 36 rows to 4in (10cm) in patt on No. 6 (4½mm) needles.

Hat

Using set of four No. 6 (4½mm) needles cast on 104 sts.
1st and 2nd rounds *K1, P1, rep from * to end.
3rd round K to end.
4th round P to end.
Rep these 4 rounds until work measures 11¾in (30cm); end with a 2nd round.

Shape top

1st round *K23, sl 1, K2 tog, psso, rep from * to end. Patt 3 rounds.
5th round *K21, sl 1, K2 tog, psso, rep from * to end.
Cont to dec in this way on every 4th round twice more, then on every alternate round until 16 sts rem. Cut off yarn, thread through sts, pull to gather and fasten off.
Note: When dec on a ribbing round, work sl 1, K2 tog, psso OR P3 tog, according to patt.

Scarf

Using No. 6 (4½mm) needles cast on 45 sts.
1st row K1, *P1, K1, rep from * to end.
2nd row P1, *K1, P1, rep from * to end.
3rd and 4th rows K to end.
Rep these 4 rows until work measures 67in (170cm); end with a 2nd row. Bind off. Run a thread through each end of scarf and pull to gather.
Make 2 pompoms, about 3¼in (8cm) in diameter, and sew one to each end.

Right glove

Using set of four No. 3 (3¼mm) needles cast on 48 sts. Work in rounds of K1, P1 ribbing for 2¼in (6cm). Change to four No. 5 (4mm) needles. Cont in rounds of patt as for hat, shaping as foll:
1st and 2nd rounds P1, K3, P1, patt to end.
3rd round P1, K1, pick up loop lying between needles and K tbl—called make 1 (M1)—, K1, M1, K1, P1, patt to end.
4th and 5th rounds P1, K5, P1, patt to end.
6th round P1, K1, M1, K3, M1, K1, P1, patt to end.
Keeping thumb sts in stockinette st and main part in patt, cont to inc on every 3rd round until there are 62 sts. Work 3 rounds. Working main part in patt and fingers and thumb in stockinette st, cont as for man's gloves from *** to end, making all fingers ¼in (5mm) shorter than man's.

*Quilting
*Hand quilting
*Frog fastenings
*Chinese ball buttons
*Pattern for a quilted jacket:
 adapting the pattern;
 directions for making

Quilting

Quilting is a distinctive technique in which two or more thicknesses of fabric are stitched together in a planned design. Quilted garments are lightweight and warm and can be made to look either elegant or sporty.

The main fabric should be a pliable, soft material like cotton, flannel or silk. A thicker padding fabric, known as batting or fiberfill, is stitched to the wrong side of the main fabric to produce a soft, puffed effect. There are several kinds of batting, but polyester is most suitable as it is light, washable and springy. In addition to the main fabric and batting, you will need a fairly firm and closely woven material such as chambray, lawn, muslin or poplin; occasionally, a lining fabric is used for the backing when the garment is not separately lined. It is best to quilt the fabric before cutting out the main pattern pieces. If this is not possible because the cloth is too bulky, allow extra material (about 2in [5cm]) all around each pattern piece before cutting. This extra fabric will be taken up in the quilting and any excess can be trimmed during the assembling.

The designs for quilting can be formal or informal. Small freehand motifs are attractive quilted on specific areas of a

plain background, such as a pocket, sleeve or yoke. On the Chinese silk jacket featured here, we have followed the design of the fabric. When using a machine for stitching intricately curved designs, mount the work in an embroidery hoop, remove the presser foot and set the machine for free embroidery. On the cotton jacket, we have quilted simple straight lines using an adjustable

quilting guide on the machine. The most common quilting designs are squares, diamonds and evenly spaced straight lines, which are easy to make without marking out the design first. If the design is more intricate, mark it with tailor's chalk, basting, soft washable pencil or pouncing (holes are pricked along the paper design and colored chalk is then rubbed through to the fabric).

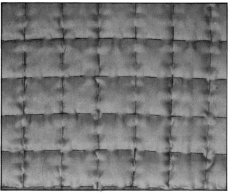

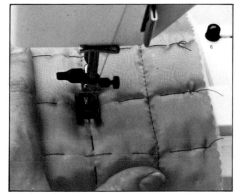

1 For either geometric or patterned quilting, prepare the fabric by pressing it to remove any creases. Transfer the design to the right of the top fabric using a suitable method for the fabric. Use a cardboard pattern if the design is a repeating one.

2 Lay the backing fabric on a flat surface, wrong side up. Lay the batting on top and the main fabric on the batting (with right side up). Baste carefully through all three layers to hold, first across the center area, then in a grid formation.

3 Geometric designs are easier to work on a machine. Attach an adjustable quilting guide or edge marker to the machine and set to the width required. Use the edge of the marker as a guide for the next quilting line.

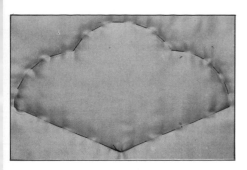

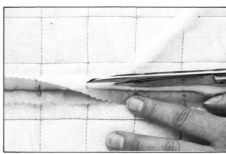

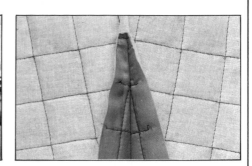

If the quilting is to follow a complicated pattern, the main design lines should be basted on first through all thicknesses. The grid basting can be removed before stitching in this case.

4 The quilting is easier to do, and will lie flatter, if you start in the center of the piece to be quilted and work out.

5 To reduce the thickness of the seam allowance after the seam has been stitched, trim away the batting from the seam allowance as close to the stitching as possible. The seam can now be pressed open.

6 To reduce the bulkiness of darts, slit the dart almost to the point. Trim away some of the batting layers on each side and press the dart open.

Hand quilting

The preparation for hand quilting is the same as for machine quilting, and the same fabrics are used, though generally a thinner batting, such as a lightweight polyester fiberfill, would be chosen. Hand quilting is suitable for small areas and for awkward places or designs. As with machine quilting, all ends of threads should be taken to the back of the work and fastened off securely.

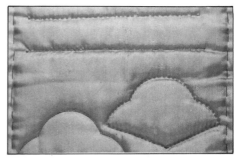

1 After marking out the design, baste all layers in a grid formation. Use a rectangular quilting or tapestry frame to mount the work if the piece is large enough; if not, a small embroidery hoop is suitable, but anything to stretch the work taut can be used.

2 There are two basic stitches used for hand quilting. Back stitch is generally used where the reverse side is lined or where a strong stitch is required to hold the layers. Stab stitch (a single running stitch) is used if the reverse side is to show, such as on an unlined jacket. Make sure the stitches are even in length.

Frog fastenings

Frog fastenings are a decorative feature found mostly on Oriental, Russian and military-style clothing. They can be made from fine cord, fabric tubing or braid and are usually used with ball buttons. A frog can be made in any size and can have as many loops as necessary to make up the design. Make one frog to the required size, then take it apart to calculate the length of braid needed for the frog fastenings, noting that each fastening will have two frogs.

1 Make the first loop the size and shape needed and sew in place, using a few small, firm stitches to hold the end down.

2 Make a second loop next to the first, taking the cord back over the original joining and sew it in place, using firm stitches as before. The loops should be of equal size.

continued

3 The third and fourth loops are made in the same way and sewn in place. The last loop is usually made slightly longer and sewn together almost to the end, leaving a big enough loop to fit over the button on the corresponding frog.

4 The frog which is to have the ball button will have the long loop sewn together all along and the button sewn to the end. Alternately, make ball buttons, leaving enough braid at each end to make all the loops needed for the frog.

5 When each frog is completed, it should be sewn to the garment by hand. The loop and the button ends should meet over the opening edges of the garment. The remaining frog loops should be sewn to the garment using small invisible slip stitches all around.

Chinese ball buttons

These knotted buttons are used with frog fastenings and can be made with narrow cord, corded tubing or braid. Make a sample button to see how much cord is needed. Add this measurement to the frog length if you are making all-in-one buttons and frogs. The thicker the cord, the bigger the button.

1 Cut a length of cord. Make a loop, bringing the cord counter-clockwise and down to the right.

2 Take the cord back over counter-clockwise between the loop and the cord end.

3 Holding the first loops firmly in one hand, take the cord through the top loop.

4 Still holding the loops, push the cord up between the gap where the loops cross.

5 Take the cord over the top loop and down through the bottom loop. Pull the ends tightly to form the button. Either cut off the ends and sew them behind the button, or make into frog fastenings as described above.

62

Quilted jacket

This versatile jacket will look exotic in traditional silk, or practical and pretty in cotton. The quilting will keep you warm and the optional pockets are roomy.

Adapting the pattern

The jacket is made by adapting the pattern for the basic shirt from the Stitch by Stitch Pattern Pack, available in sizes 10-20, corresponding to sizes 8-18 in ready-made clothes.

Materials
3 sheets of tracing paper 36 x 40in
  (90 x 100cm approx)
Flexible curve
Yardstick

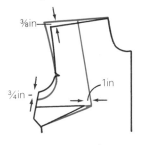

1 Pin the front yoke to the shirt front and the back yoke to the shirt back, overlapping the $\frac{5}{8}$in (1.5cm) seam allowances so that the seams are aligned. Trace both complete pieces.

2 To make the jacket front pattern, square the shoulder line by measuring up and out $\frac{3}{8}$in (1cm) from the shoulder point cutting lines and draw the new shoulder cutting line, tapering into the cutting line at the neck edge.

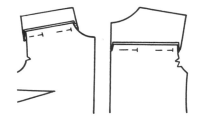

3 Drop the armhole at the side seam by measuring down from the armhole cutting line $\frac{3}{4}$in (2cm) and mark. Using a flexible curve, re-draw the armhole by connecting the new shoulder cutting line to the mark at the side seam.

4 The bust dart allowance is moved to the shoulder: mark the center of the shoulder seam, extend the top bust dart line by 1in (2.5cm) and re-draw lower bust dart line to this point. Draw a line from the mark at the shoulder to this point.

Ross Greetham

5/8 in

5 Cut along the line from the shoulder to the bust point. Close the side bust dart and tape in place. This will open the pattern at the shoulder. Tape a piece of paper under opening. Add a 5/8in (1.5cm) seam allowance to both edges of dart.

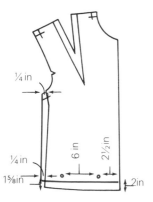

1/4 in
1/4 in
1 5/8 in
6 in
2 1/2 in
2 in

6 To mark the jacket length, measure up from lower edge of pattern 2in (5cm) at the center front edge and 1 5/8in (4cm) at the side seam. Draw a line across the pattern: this will be the new hem cutting line. A 5/8in (1.5cm) seam allowance has been included in these measurements.

7 To allow more ease across the bust and hips, measure out from the side cutting line 1/4in (6mm) at new underarm curve and 1/4in (6mm) at hem edge. Draw the new side cutting line connecting these points. Mark the seam allowance.

8 For the pocket position, measure in along the new hemline from center front edge 2 1/2in (6.5cm) and mark. Measure in a further 6in (15cm) from this point and mark. The bottom edge of the pocket will be positioned between these points.

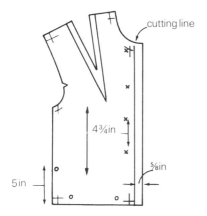

cutting line
4 3/4 in
5/8 in
5 in

John Hutchinson

9 Mark length of side slit 5in (13cm) up from the lower edge on the side seam. Trim away 5/8in (1.5cm) all along center.

Victor Yuan

front edge. The trimmed edge will be the cutting line. Mark ⅝in (1.5cm) seamlines and grain line parallel to the front edge.

10 Mark the fastening positions on the front seamline. Place the first at the neck seamline on the front edge and the others at regular intervals along the seamline. The jacket shown here has four fastenings at 4¾in (12cm) intervals.

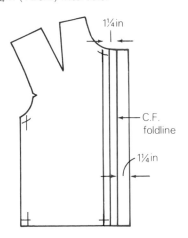

11 To make the front bands, lay paper over the front edge of the jacket front and trace the new seamline from the neck to the hem edge and part of the neck cutting line. Measure out 1¼in (3cm) from the traced line all down the center front and draw a line. This will be the center front and grain line.

12 Draw another line 1¼in (3cm) away from and parallel to center front line. This will be the front band facing cutting line.

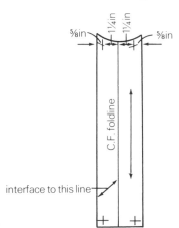

13 Fold the band in half along the foldline and trace the neck curve to the other half of the band. Add ⅝in (1.5cm) seam allowance to each long edge of the band. Mark the grain line parallel to the foldline or on the center front line.

14 To make the jacket back pattern, follow the directions and measurements for the jacket front and square the shoulder line. Drop the armhole at the side seam. Mark the jacket length and allow for more ease across the bust and hips as before. Mark seamline and indicate that center back is on a fold.

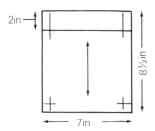

15 To make the pocket pattern, draw a rectangle 8½ x 7in (22 x 18cm). Mark the foldline 2in (5cm) from the top edge and seam allowances ⅝in (1.5cm) in from the side and lower edges. Mark the grain line parallel to the side edge.

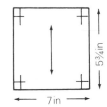

16 To make pocket lining pattern, draw a rectangle 5¾in (14.5cm) deep by 7in (18cm) wide. Mark ⅝in (1.5cm) seam allowance on all edges and grain line parallel to side edges.

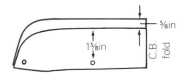

17 To make the collar pattern, trace the stand collar pattern. Make the finished width of collar 1⅝in (4cm). Re-draw the top cutting line of the collar ⅝in (1.5cm) out from the original cutting line, curving the line at the front edge.

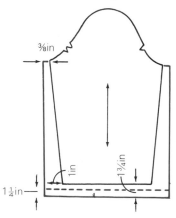

18 To make the sleeve pattern, trace the shirt sleeve pattern and mark the grain line. To adjust the sleeve length, add 1¾in (4.5cm) to lower edge of sleeve and draw a line across for the cutting line. Mark the hem foldline 1¼in (3cm) up from the new hem cutting line.

19 To allow for ease in the sleeve, measure out from both underarm cutting lines 1in (2.5cm) from lower edge and

⅜in (1cm) at underarm curve. Connect these lines for new underarm cutting lines.

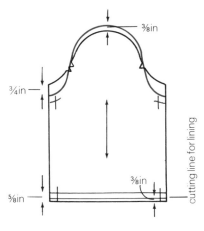

John Hutchinson

20 Drop the underarm curves of the sleeve cap by measuring down the new underarm seamline from the sleeve cap cutting line ¾in (2cm) and mark. Raise the center of the sleeve cap ⅜in (1cm) and using a flexible curve, re-draw both sides of the sleeve cap from the center point to the mark at the underarm seams, crossing the original cutting line at the notches.

21 Mark the ⅝in (1.5cm) seam allowance and the grain line. For the cutting line, measure up from lower edge ⅜in (1cm) and draw a line across the pattern. A ⅝ (1.5cm) seam allowance has been included at lower edge of the lining.

Directions for making

Suggested fabrics

Poplin, jacquard weave silk, pinwale corduroy, velvet, velveteen, satin, lawn, polyester/cotton blend, wool/cotton blend flannel. Lining: silk, cotton, polyester. Batting: polyester fiberfill.

Materials

36in (90cm)-wide fabric with or without nap:
Sizes 10 to 16: 2⅝yd (2.4m)
Sizes 18, 20: 2¾yd (2.5m)
Note: The above yardages do not allow for matching large patterns; allow for this when buying fabric.
36in (90cm)-wide lining fabric with or without nap:
Sizes 10 to 14: 2½yd (2.2m)
Sizes 16 to20: 2⅝yd (2.3m)
36in (90cm)-wide batting: follow lining layout and yardage for size
36in (90cm)-wide interfacing: for all sizes ¾yd (.7m)
Matching thread
Enough cord or braid to make frogs and buttons, or piping cord and fabric loops with toggles. (The jacket on page 63 takes ⅝yd [50cm] of 36in [90cm]-wide fabric, 2¼yd [2m] piping cord.)
4 toggles
Shoulder pads

Cutting layout for 36in-wide fabric with or without nap

fold

(for view 2 omit the pocket)

selvages

36in-wide lining

fold

selvages

(for view 2 omit the pocket)

36in-wide interfacing

fold

selvages

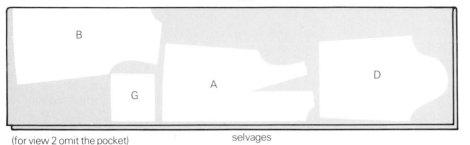

Key to adjusted pattern pieces

A Jacket front — Cut 2
B Jacket back — Cut 1 on fold
C Front bands — Cut 2
D Sleeve — Cut 2
E Collar — Cut 2 on fold
F Pocket — Cut 2
Lining: use pieces
G Pocket lining — Cut 2
A Front — Cut 2
B Back — Cut 1 on fold
D Sleeve — Cut 2
Interfacing: use pieces E Cut 1 on fold,
C Cut 2 to half width only

Terry Evans

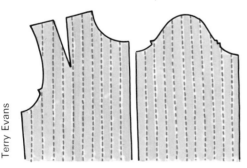

1 Prepare the fabric for quilting as shown on page 60 and quilt by hand or machine according to the design, following the directions on page 60. If using vertical quilting, keep the lines parallel to the straight grain and spaced approximately 1¼in (3cm) apart.
2 When the quilting is completed and the pattern pieces trimmed, fold, baste and stitch the front shoulder darts of the jacket and the lining. Trim the batting close to the stitching and press open (see page 61)

3 With right sides together, baste and stitch the pocket lining to pocket along top edge, taking a ⅝in (1.5cm) seam. Press seam allowance toward lining.

4 With right sides together, fold the pocket along the foldline and baste and stitch around the side and lower edges, leaving 2in (5cm) open at the bottom. Trim seams and clip corners.
5 Turn the pocket right side out through the opening. Turn in the seam allowance at the opening and slip stitch to close. Baste around the outer edges of the pocket and press flat.

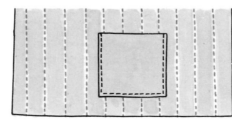

6 Baste the pockets to the jacket fronts in position indicated on the pattern.

Topstitch pockets in place, stitching ¼in (6mm) in from the edges.

7 With right sides together, baste and stitch the shoulder seams and side seams of the jacket, leaving the lower part of the side seams open for the slit openings. Trim the batting as shown on page 61 and press open. Do the same with the lining fronts and back.
8 With right sides together, baste and stitch the underarm seam of the sleeve. Trim the batting and press the seam open. Repeat with other sleeve and sleeve linings.

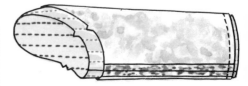

9 With right sides together, slip the lining over the sleeve. Matching seams, baste and stitch the lining to the sleeve around lower edge, taking ⅝in (1.5cm) seam. Trim the batting and press the seam allowances toward the lining.

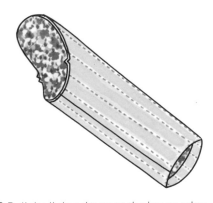

10 Pull the lining down to the lower edge of the sleeve, then fold the sleeve along the hemline and push the lining back inside the sleeve. Baste around the hem edge and press gently.

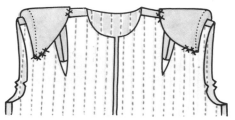

11 Sew the shoulder pads inside of the jacket, catch stitching them to the shoulder line and armhole seamline on each side (see Volume 9, page 61).

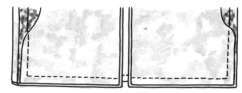

12 With right sides together and side seams matching, baste and stitch the lining to the jacket along the front and back hem edges and around each side slit, taking $\frac{5}{8}$ (1.5cm) seams. Grade the seams and clip across corners.

13 Turn the lining right side out, pressing the seam allowance toward the jacket. With wrong sides together, baste the lining to the jacket around the armhole, neck and front edges.

14 With right sides together and shoulder points and seams matching, pin and baste the sleeve into the armhole. Stitch all around, working with the sleeve facing up on the machine and keeping the sleeve lining clear of the stitching. Trim the batting, trim seam and press toward sleeve. Overcast seams together and clip underarm curves.

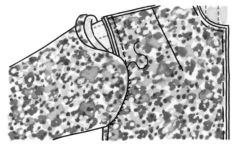

15 Bring the sleeve lining up over the sleeve. Turn under the seam allowance around the sleeve cap of the lining and slip stitch to the armhole stitching line, enclosing all raw edges. Press and repeat with other sleeve.

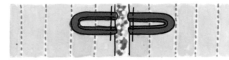

16 If making loop-and-toggle fastenings as an alternative to frogs, cut or make $3\frac{1}{2}$in (9cm) lengths of cord or corded tubing (see Volume 1, page 57). Fold loops in half and stitch on seamline to front edges of jacket (made as for button loops: see Volume 1, page 62).

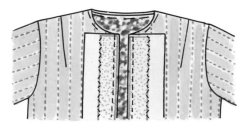

17 Baste interfacing to the wrong side of the top sides of the front bands and catch stitch interfacing to the foldline. With right sides together, baste and stitch the front bands to the jacket fronts. Grade the seam allowances, trimming interfacing and batting close to the stitching.

18 Fold the bands along the foldline with right sides together and stitch across the lower edge of the bands from the folded edge to the seamline. Trim seams and clip corners.

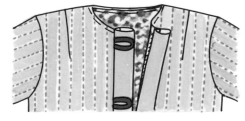

19 Turn the bands right side out and baste along folded edges. On the inside of the garment, turn under the seam allowance along the inner edge of the bands and slip stitch to the stitching line. Press.

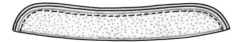

20 Baste interfacing to the wrong side of top collar. With right sides together, baste and stitch the two collar sections together, leaving the neck edge open. Trim the seam allowance, trimming the interfacing close to the stitching. Turn collar right side out and baste around stitched edge. Press.

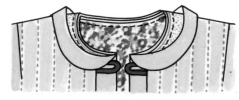

21 With right sides together and center backs, shoulder points and center fronts matching, baste and stitch the interfaced edge of the collar to the neck edge. Grade seam, trimming interfacing close to stitching. Clip around curves. Press seam allowance toward collar.

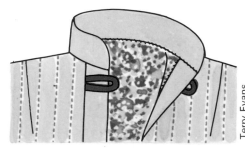

22 On the inside of the jacket turn under the $\frac{5}{8}$ (1.5cm) seam allowance of under collar and slip stitch it to stitching line around neck edge. Remove all basting and press carefully from the wrong side.

23 Make frog fastenings (two parts to each fastening) and one Chinese ball button for each as shown on page 62. Sew frogs to each jacket front in chosen positions, with the first fastening close to the top edge. Or, sew toggles or buttons to loops on left front jacket.

Terry Evans

*Working with skins and
 leather-like fabrics
*Cut-work motifs on
 non-fraying fabrics
*Pattern for a vest and skirt:
 adapting the patterns;
 directions for making

Working with skins and leather-like fabrics

When making a garment in suede or leather, it is advisable to make the garment in muslin first and fit it before cutting the skin. All necessary adjustments can be made on the muslin shell and the pattern altered before marking the skin.

Leather skins are sold by the square measure with the average sheepskin about 1 square yard (or meter) in size. As you must pay for the whole skin, it is useful to lay out the pattern pieces on the skins to see where they need to be joined, and to estimate amounts needed. The center of leather skins is often thicker than the edges and, since it is best to avoid using different thicknesses in one pattern piece, cut from the center of the skin for the main parts of the garment. Suede has a nap, so all the pattern pieces should be laid in the same direction, with the nap

running downward. The direction of the nap can be found by brushing the suede, as with velvet and other napped fabrics. Before cutting out, lay the skins flat and cut each piece separately, reversing pieces placed on a fold where necessary. Needles and pins leave permanent holes, so be careful when using them. For machine stitching, use heavy-duty silk or mercerized cotton and a wedge-point needle, which is designed especially for stitching leather and should be replaced as soon as it becomes blunt. Adjust the stitch length and pressure of the presser foot of the sewing machine to suit the thickness of the seam, and, if possible, use a special roller or non-stick foot for stitching leather fabrics.

Suedes or leather-like fabrics should be treated in the same way as skins, with

the exception of vinyl fabrics, which should not be glued (a technique used for seams on leather garments). Instead, use topstitching, hand sewing or careful pressing to hold seams, hems and facings in place.

Where two seams cross and form extra bulk, as on a yoke line crossing over an underarm seam, or on armhole and underarm seams, the excess thickness should be trimmed away from the seam allowance underlayers before gluing down the top layers. Occasionally leather will be too thick at the seam even if trimmed, so the excess can be shaved from the back of the seam allowance with a sharp craft knife or razor blade. When shaving leather, be very careful to avoid cutting right through the hem or seam allowance.

1 Avoid using too many pins; pin inside the seam allowance or use transparent tape to hold the pattern in place. Use sharp scissors for cutting.

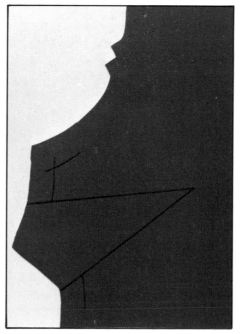

2 Cut all notches outward or mark them with tailor's chalk on the wrong side. Mark darts and other pattern lines on the wrong side with chalk.

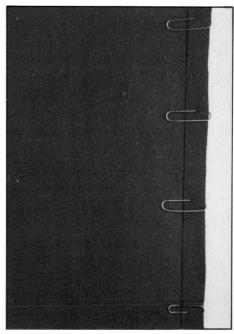

3 If possible, avoid basting the pieces together, as this will mark skins. Use tape, paper clips or clothespins to hold the seam allowances together, and remove them individually when stitching. If basting is necessary, be sure to baste inside the seam allowances so the marks do not show.

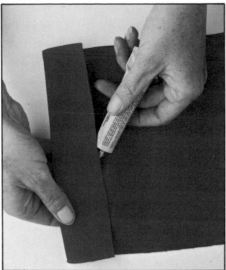

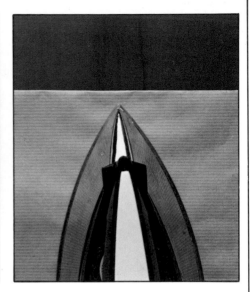

4 Grade the seams on the inside of collars, cuffs and facing, pockets and waistbands in the usual way, gluing down the allowances afterward.

5 To prevent facings and seams from rolling out of place, glue the seam allowance or facing in place with rubber cement. Spread the glue on the underside of the seam allowance and press the seam against the garment with your fingertip. If using vinyl, understitch or topstitch the facings to prevent rolling.

6 Cut through the center of darts and press them open. Glue down the allowance on each side. Seams should be pressed carefully on the wrong side with a warm iron over a dry press cloth, or over a sheet of clean brown paper. Flatten seams with a rolling pin or mallet after stitching.

Cutwork motifs

This type of decoration is most suitable for a fabric or material which does not fray, such as suede, leather, leather-like fabric, plastic and vinyl. On the outfit on page 70, cutwork motifs are used on the front, yoke and skirt hem but could be used on garments with sleeves, bodices and pockets or on evening bags. The technique involves stitching around the outline to be cut out before actually cutting the shape.

On fabrics which fray, it is possible to get a similar effect by stitching around the outline using a short zig-zag stitch, which finishes the raw edges as well as strengthening them. For extra effect, the cut-out sections may be backed with a lining fabric in a matching or contrasting color: cut a strip to go behind the cut-out section, turn edges under and slip stitch in place.

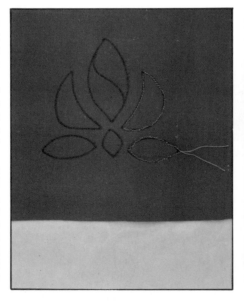

Simon Butcher

1 Mark the design on the wrong side of the piece to be cut out, using tailor's chalk or suitable marker. Working from the wrong side, stitch all around the marked motifs without breaking the stitching line if possible (adjust machine for free embroidery and use an embroidery hoop). To prevent marking napped fabrics, place tissue paper between fabric and machine plate.

2 Secure the ends of the stitching on the wrong side by tying the ends or stitching in. Using small, sharp scissors or a craft knife, cut out the center of each motif as close to the stitching line as possible. Keep the work flat and work on a hard, smooth surface.

Suede vest and skirt

Stylized cutwork motifs and harmonizing braid trim give this simple outfit an air of haute couture. Any rich color would look as good as the green suede used here.

Jean Claude Volpelière

Adapting the patterns

The vest and skirt are made by adapting the pattern for the basic shirt and skirt patterns taken from the Stitch by Stitch Pattern Pack, available in sizes 10 to 20, corresponding to sizes 8-18 in ready-made clothes.

Materials

4 sheets of tracing paper 36×40in (approx. 90×100cm)
Flexible curve, yardstick

Vest

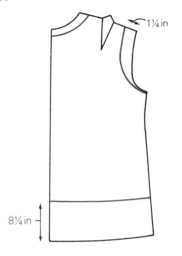

1 To make the vest back pattern, trace the jacket back pattern, leaving extra paper at the center back edge. Omit the back neck seam allowance. The seamline will now be the cutting line. To mark the length of the vest, measure up from lower edge 8¼in (21cm) and draw new cutting line across pattern. This includes a ⅝in (1.5cm) hem.

2 Measure in from the armhole cutting line along the shoulder line 1¼in (3cm) and mark. Using a flexible curve, draw the new armhole cutting line from this mark to the original seamline at the underarm.

3 To make the yoke pattern, measure down the center back line from the back neck edge 4½in (11.5cm) for sizes 10, 12; 4¾in (12cm) for sizes 14, 16; 5in (12.5cm) for sizes 18, 20. Draw a line across the pattern to the armhole at this point. Extend the shoulder dart lines down to meet the yoke line as shown.

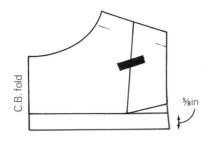

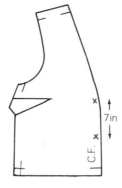

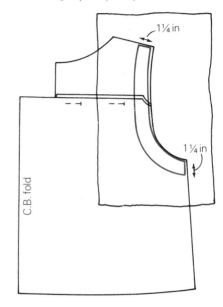

pattern, trace the armhole edge and along the shoulder and side cutting lines 1¼in (3cm). Using a flexible curve, connect up the points at the shoulder and side, keeping the facing parallel to the armhole edge all around. The facing should be 1¼in (3cm) deep.

4 Cut along the yoke line to separate the yoke pattern from the back. Close the shoulder dart and tape in place. Straighten the bottom line of the yoke and add ⅝in (1.5cm) for the seam allowance. Mark the center back to be placed on a fold.

8 For the tie positions at the front edge put the first mark level with the bust dart and the second mark 7in (18cm) below first mark.

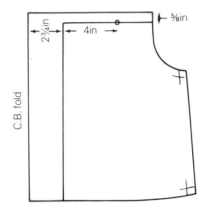

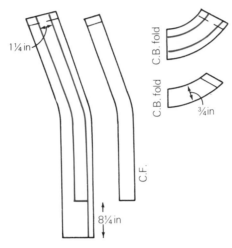

11 To make the back armhole facing pattern, pin the back yoke to the vest back along the seamline. Trace the armhole edge and draft the facing following directions given for the front armhole facing.
The facing should be 1¼in (3cm) deep all around the curve of the armhole, as for the neck and front edges.

5 Mark in the gathering position along the yoke seamline on the back pattern—it will be 4in (10cm) in from center back. Add 2¾in (7cm) all along center back of the jacket for the gathering allowance. Add ⅝in (1.5cm) seam allowance to the top edge of the back.

9 To make the front and back neck facing pattern, trace the front and back jacket neck facings, omitting the neck edge seam allowance. The seamlines will be the cutting lines, except on the shoulder where ⅝in (1.5cm) seam allowances are needed. Shorten the front neck facing by 8¼in (21cm) and make both facing pattern pieces 1¼in (3cm) wide.

Skirt

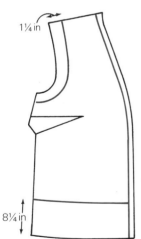

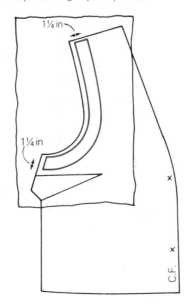

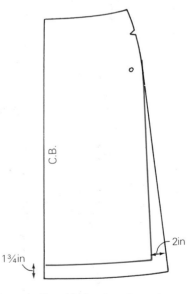

6 To make the vest front pattern, trace the jacket front pattern omitting the seam allowance on the front edge. The seamline will be the cutting line. Mark the length 8¼in (21cm) up from lower edge and draw a line across pattern. A ⅝in (1.5cm) hem has been included.
7 Measure in from the armhole cutting line along the shoulder line 1¼in (3cm) and mark. Draw the new armhole cutting line from mark to underarm seamline.

10 To make the front armhole facing

1 To make the skirt back pattern, trace the skirt back pattern, leaving extra paper at the center back edge and omitting the dart lines. The dart allowance will be included in the gathering. Measure up from lower edge 1¾in (4.5cm) and draw new cutting line across pattern.

2 At the lower edge, measure in along the new cutting line from the side cutting line 2in (5cm) and mark. Using a yardstick, draw the new side cutting line from this point, tapering into the original line at the hip line. Mark in the ⅝in (1.5cm) seam allowance.

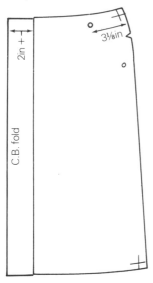

3 For the gathering position, measure in 3⅛in (8cm) along the waist seamline from the side cutting line and mark. Add an allowance for the gathering to the center back edge 2in (5cm) for a size 10, adding an extra ¾in (2cm) to this measurement for each larger size.

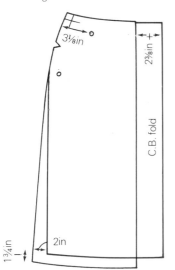

4 To make the skirt front pattern, trace the skirt front pattern, omitting the dart lines. The dart allowance will be included in the gathering. Following directions given for altering the skirt back pattern, shorten the skirt length by 1¾in (4.5cm) and narrow it at the side hem by 2in (5cm).

5 Mark the gathering position 3⅛in (8cm) in from side cutting line. Add 2⅜in (6cm) at center front for gathering allowance for a size 10, adding ¾in (2cm) to this measurement for each larger size.

Directions for making

Suggested fabrics

Suede, leather, leather-like fabric, vinyl, velvet, velveteen. If omitting cutwork, any medium-weight fabric such as wool flannel, pinwale corduroy, crepe.

Materials

54in (140cm)-wide fabric with or without nap:
    Sizes 10, 12: 2½yd (2.2m)
    Size 14: 2⅝yd (2.4m)
    Sizes 16, 18, 20: 3yd (3.7m)
36in (90cm)-wide fabric with or without nap:
    Sizes 10-14: 3⅜yd (3m)
    Sizes 16-20: 3½yd (3.2m)
36in (90cm)-wide interfacing:
    Sizes 10 to 18: 6in (15cm)
    Size 20: 10in (25cm)
Matching thread, glue or rubber cement
7in (18cm) skirt zipper, skirt hook and eye
3⅜yd (3m) braid for sizes 10-14
3⅞yd (3.5m) braid for sizes 16-20

Key to adjusted pattern pieces

A	Vest front	Cut 2
B	Vest back	Cut 1 on fold
C	Vest back yoke	Cut 1 on fold
D	Front neck facing	Cut 2
E	Back neck facing	Cut 1 on fold
F	Front armhole facing	Cut 2
G	Back armhole facing	Cut 2
H	Skirt front	Cut 1 on fold
I	Skirt back	Cut 1 on fold
J	Waistband	Cut 1

John Hutchinson

Cutting layout for 54in-wide fabric with or without nap: Sizes 10/14

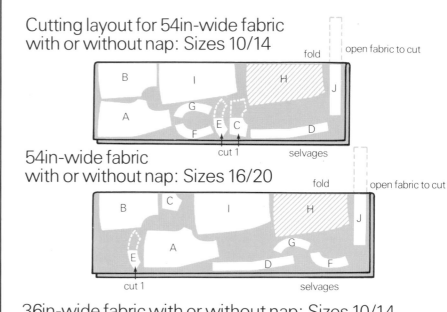

54in-wide fabric with or without nap: Sizes 16/20

36in-wide fabric with or without nap: Sizes 10/14

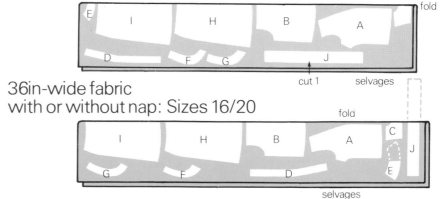

36in-wide fabric with or without nap: Sizes 16/20

Vest

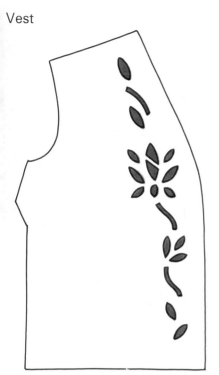

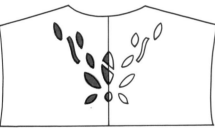

1 Transfer the motif design to the wrong side of the vest fronts and back yoke with tailor's chalk. Stitch around the design and cut out the centers of the design close to the stitching as shown on page 69.

2 With right sides together, fold, baste and stitch the bust darts. Cut through the center of the darts and press open. Glue down the dart allowance on each side.

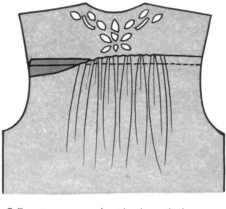

3 Run two rows of gathering stitches on the seamline of the yoke edge of the back between the marked circles.
Pull up the gathering threads until the back fits the yoke. Pin and baste or clip the back to the yoke, spreading the gathers evenly. Stitch the seam.
4 Remove the gathering threads. Trim the yoke seam allowance, press the seam allowance toward the yoke and glue down.

5 With right sides together, stitch the shoulder and side seams of vest. Press seams open and glue down. Trim away the side seam allowance within the ⅝in (1.5cm) hem allowance.

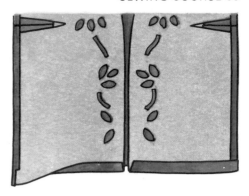

6 Turn up the ⅝in (1.5cm) allowance at the hem and glue or stitch in place with a row of machine stitching about ⅜in (1cm) from the folded edge.

7 Cut four lengths of braid each 10in (25cm) long and eight leaf shapes from leather or fabric. To make the four ties, insert one end of each length of braid between two leaf shapes and glue together over the end of the braid. Stitch all around close to the edge to hold.

8 Glue the end of each tie to the wrong side of the front edges in the position indicated on the pattern. Stitch over the ties ¼in (6mm) from the edge to hold.

9 With right sides together, stitch the front and back armhole facings together at the shoulder and side seams. Press all seams open and glue down.

10 With right sides together, stitch the front and back neck facings together at the shoulder seams. Press seams open and glue down.

11 Trim ⅝in (1.5cm) from hem edge of front neck facings. With wrong sides together and matching seams, glue the armhole facings to the armhole edges, and the neck facings to the neck edges. Press flat. Stitch ⅛in (3mm) from edges all around if necessary to hold in place.

Terry Evans

Jean Claude Volnelière

LEAF SHAPE
FOR TIES

cut 8

John Hutchinson

12 Cut a piece of braid to fit around the front and back neck and center front. Position the braid close to the edge of these and stitch in place with one row of machine stitching, turning in raw ends of braid. If necessary, use narrow zig-zag stitch.

Skirt

1 Transfer the motif design to the wrong side of the skirt front and back at the hem edge, allowing ¾in (2cm) clearance when

hem is turned up. Stitch around the design and cut out the centers close to the stitching.

2 With right sides together, stitch the side seams, leaving an opening for the zipper at the left side seam. Press the seam open and glue down seam allowance.

3 Insert zipper into the side seam opening as directed for basic skirt. The zipper can be stitched in place by machine, or by hand using stabstitch.

4 Run two rows of gathering stitches between the gathering positions on the

front and back waist. Glue the interfacing to the wrong side of the waistband or catch-stitch in place on the foldline.

5 With right sides together, pin the waistband to the skirt, pulling up the gathers of the skirt to fit the waistband. Spread the gathers evenly across the front and back and stitch the seam.

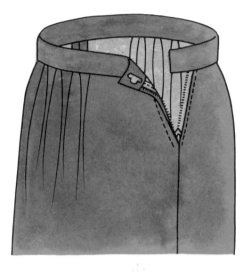

6 Trim the waistband seam allowance. Press the allowances toward the waistband and glue down. Complete waistband as directed for basic skirt. Glue the waistband down on the inside if using suede or leather, or slip stitch if using leather-like fabrics. Sew hook and eye to waistband at the top of the side opening.

7 Trim the side seam allowance within the hem allowance. Turn ¾in (2cm) hem allowance to the inside and glue down or stitch in place.

Note: If desired, braid can be stitched to the hem edges of the skirt and vest, and the armhole edges for extra decoration. Allow extra yardage.

Terry Evans

Handy shopping bag

Made in bright vinyl fabric, this useful tote bag will carry shopping, library books—whatever you like.

Finished size
Approx 19×12½in (48×32cm).
A seam allowance of ¾in (2cm) has been included throughout.

Materials
⅞yd (.8m) of 54in (140cm)-wide
   vinyl fabric
Paper for pattern
Matching thread
Piece of cardboard 12½×4½in
   (32×11.5cm)
Fabric glue
Paper clips; ruler
Transparent tape

1 To make the paper pattern for the bag, draw a rectangle 23×20in (60×51cm) on a sheet of paper.
2 For the base corners, measure in 3in (8cm) along lower edge of rectangle from one corner and mark, then measure up the side 2¼in (6cm) from the same corner and mark. Draw two intersecting lines from these marks. Repeat at the opposite corner. Cut out pattern, cutting out both corners.
3 Fold vinyl in half to measure 31½×27in (80×70cm). Place the pattern on the vinyl with base edge on the fold. Hold pattern in place with paper clips. Cut out bag.
4 Cut two pieces of vinyl, each 20×5½in (50×14cm), for handles.
5 Fold bag in half with right sides together and sides matching. Hold sides in place with paper clips and tape. Stitch side seams.
6 Pull out base fold and match to raw edges of sides. Hold edges in place with paper clips and tape. Stitch sides to base. Trim seam and turn bag right side out.
7 At the top edge turn ¾in (2cm) to the wrong side. Turn under another ¾in (2cm) to form a double hem. Hold the hem in place with paper clips and tape. Topstitch around the top of the bag, close to the hem edge.
8 Fold bag along sides, 2¼in (6cm) in from side seam and topstitch along the sides and base, close to folded edges.
9 Turn in ¾in (2cm) on all four edges of one handle, then fold the handle in half lengthwise. Hold edges in place with paper clips and tape. Topstitch all around handle, ⅜in from the edge.
10 Repeat step 9 to make the other handle in the same way.

Tom Leighton

11 Place one handle on one side of bag, with handle ends 4¼in (11cm) in from the sides and 2¼in (6cm) down from the top. Hold handle in place with tape. Topstitch the handle ends in place, stitching over original stitching lines and then crossing from corner to corner.
12 Repeat step 11 to stitch the other

handle in place on the other side of bag.
13 For inside base cut a piece of vinyl measuring 14×6in (36×15.5cm).
14 Glue cardboard in the center of the wrong side of the vinyl base. Fold the seam allowance over the cardboard side and glue it in place. Fit the base right side up inside the bag.

*False fly fastening
*Pattern for a hooded raincoat
 with detachable lining (1):
 adapting the pattern

False fly fastening

Although this type of fastening is similar in effect to a tab fly (see Volume 14, page 67), a different technique is used for assembling it. The garment front is made in the normal way, but has a separate fly piece stitched on afterward. Because the fly is cut separately, it can be faced with contrasting fabric for added effect as shown on the coat on page 78.

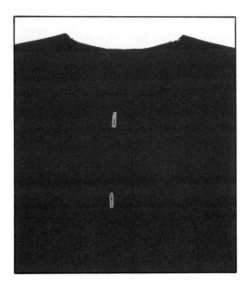

1 Finish the front edges of the garment by turning the facings to the inside in the normal way, leaving the neck edge to be completed after the fly is attached. Make the vertical buttonholes.

2 With right sides together, pin, baste and stitch the two fly pieces together, leaving the neck edge open. Trim the seam allowance and cut across the corners at the bottom edge.

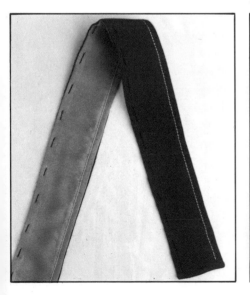

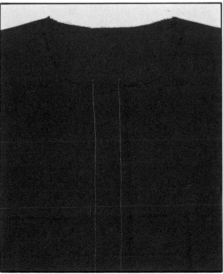

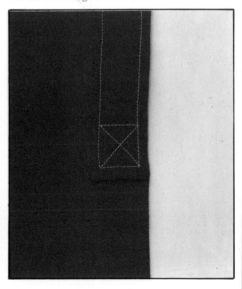

3 Turn the fly right side out and baste around the edges. Press flat. Topstitch along the outer edge of the fly piece, stitching $\frac{1}{4}$in (6mm) in from the edge to within $\frac{1}{4}$in (6mm) of the bottom edge. Pull the threads through to the wrong side and tie them securely.

4 Matching the outer edge of the fly piece to the outer edge of the front, and also the fly and front neck edges, baste the fly to the right side of the right front. Topstitch the fly in place, stitching from the neck edge down the inner edge only.

5 Stitch across the lower edge to make a cross as shown. Remove the basting and press gently from the right side. The outer edge is left unstitched to permit access to the buttonholes.

Simon Butcher

Hooded raincoat

The versatility of this coat speaks for itself. Here we've made it in showerproof lamé for a sparkling look, but you could choose a fabric more suitable for everyday wear.

Adapting the pattern

The coat is made by adapting the pattern for the basic shirt from the Stitch by Stitch Pattern Pack, available in sizes 10 to 20, corresponding to sizes 8 to 18 in ready-made clothes.

Materials
6 sheets of tracing paper 36×40in (approx. 90×100cm)
Flexible curve, yardstick

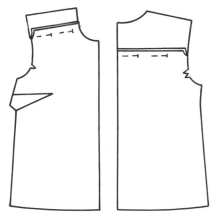

1 Pin the front yoke to the shirt front and the back yoke to the shirt back so that the seams are aligned. Trace both complete pieces, leaving extra at the center front and back edges.

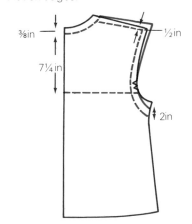

2 To make the back pattern re draw the back neck cutting line ⅜in (1cm) in from original cutting line. Square the shoulder line by measuring up and out ½in (1.2cm) from armhole seamline. Draw the new shoulder seamline, tapering into the seamline at the new neck line.

3 Lower the armhole curve at the side seam by measuring down from armhole seamline 2in (5cm) and mark. Using a flexible curve, re-draw the new armhole seamline from the shoulder line to the

Chris Harvey

side seam. Add $\frac{5}{8}$in (1.5cm) seam allowance to shoulder and armhole edges.

4 Draw a line across the pattern from the center back to the armhole edge for the back yoke, measuring down the center back from the back neck cutting line $7\frac{1}{4}$in (18.5cm) for a size 10 and adding an extra $\frac{1}{4}$in (5mm) for each larger size.

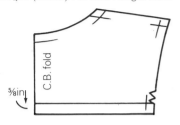

5 Cut along this line to separate the yoke. Add a $\frac{5}{8}$in (1.5cm) seam allowance to lower edge of the yoke and mark all seamlines. Indicate that center back is on a fold and that the grain line is parallel to the center back.

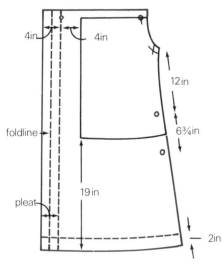

6 Add 4in (10cm) to center back edge of the back for gathers, and a further 4in (10cm) for pleat. Mark inner pleat foldline along center of 4in (10cm) allowance. To mark the length, add 19in (48cm) to the lower edge; this includes a 2in (5cm) hem allowance.

7 For the pocket position at the side seam, measure down the side seam from the armhole seamline 12in (30cm) for top of the pocket and a further $6\frac{3}{4}$in (17cm) for bottom of the pocket. Mark these points.

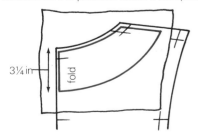

8 To make the back neck facing pattern, trace the back neck cutting line, the center back and shoulder seamline to a depth of $3\frac{1}{4}$in (8.5cm) from neck edge. Mark $\frac{5}{8}$in (1.5cm) seam allowances and indicate that center back is on a fold.

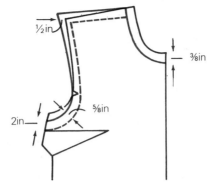

9 To make the front pattern, re-draw the front neck cutting line $\frac{3}{8}$in (1cm) in from original cutting line. Square the shoulder line by measuring up and out $\frac{1}{2}$in (1.2cm) from armhole seamline. Draw the new shoulder seamline tapering into the seamline at the new neck seamline.

10 Drop the armhole curve at the side seam by measuring down 2in (5cm) from armhole seamline. Using a flexible curve, re-draw the new armhole seamline from the new shoulder seamline to the side seam. Add $\frac{5}{8}$in (1.5cm) seam allowance to shoulder and armhole edges.

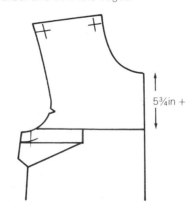

11 For the yoke line, measure down $5\frac{3}{4}$in (14.5cm) on center front from neck cutting line for a size 10, adding an extra $\frac{1}{4}$in (5mm) to this measurement for each larger size. Draw a line across the pattern at this point to the armhole edge.

12 Draw a line up to meet this line from the dart point, parallel to the center front edge.

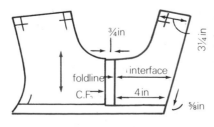

13 Cut along the yoke line to separate the yoke pattern. For the buttonhole extension, add $\frac{3}{4}$in (2cm) to center front edge and mark this as foldline. Fold the pattern along this line and trace the neck cutting line, shoulder line to $3\frac{1}{4}$in (8.5cm); and bottom yoke line to 4in (10cm).

14 Connect these two points with a straight line. This will be the outer edge of the front facing. Add $\frac{5}{8}$in (1.5cm) seam allowance to bottom edge and mark the grain line parallel to the center front. Interfacing will be cut to the foldline across the facing.

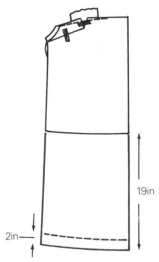

15 On the front pattern piece, cut down the drawn line to the dart point. Close the side bust dart and tape in place. This will open the pattern. Insert and tape a piece of paper behind the opening. Smooth out the sharp angle of the line at the opening. To mark length see step 6.

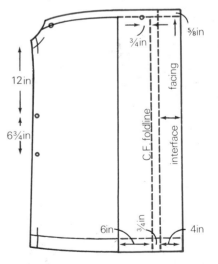

16 Add 6in (15cm) to center front edge for the gathers and mark the new center front. Add a further $\frac{3}{4}$in (2cm) for buttonhole extension and mark this as foldline. Add another 4in (10cm) for front facing. Cut interfacing to this depth.

17 Add $\frac{5}{8}$in (1.5cm) seam allowance to top edge. For gathering position measure in $\frac{3}{4}$in (2cm) from new center front and mark point. For pocket position measure down from armhole seamline 12in (30cm), then a further $6\frac{3}{4}$in (17cm), and mark.

John Hutchinson

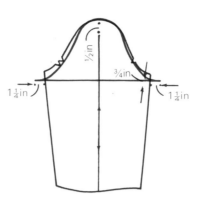

for sizes 10, 12; 9¾ × 2¾in (24.5 × 7cm) for sizes 14, 16; 10¼ × 2¾in (25.5 × 7cm) for sizes 18, 20. Measurements include a ⅝in (1.5cm) seam allowance around all edges.

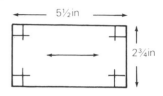

26 To make back sleeve strap pattern draw rectangle 5½ × 2¾in (14 × 7cm) for sizes 10, 12; 6 × 2¾in (15 × 7cm) for 14, 16; 6¼ × 2¾in (16 × 7cm) for 18, 20.

27 To make the pocket pattern, draw the shape of the pocket between the two marks shown, using a flexible curve. The pocket should be 7½in (19cm) deep and should slant downward.

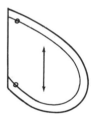

28 Trace pocket shape and mark grain line parallel to center front of garment. Add ⅝in (1.5cm) seam allowance all around curved edge.

22 To make the sleeve pattern, trace the shirt sleeve pattern, extending the grain line to the top and bottom of the sleeve. The underarm curve of the sleeve cap is lowered and at the same time the sleeve is made wider between the two underarm curves. Using a measurement of ¾in (2cm) for all sizes, drop the underarm curve, measuring down the underarm seamline from the seamline of the curve. Draw a line across the pattern at this point.
23 Raise the seamline at center of sleeve cap ½in (1.2cm) for all sizes. Extend line at underarm by 1⅛in (3cm) at each side for a size 10. See note at end of adaptations for sleeve width for other sizes. Using a flexible curve, re-draw the new sleeve cap seamline to the new underarm seams.

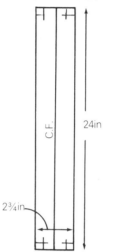

18 To make the front fly facing pattern, draw a rectangle 24in (61cm) long by 2¾in (7cm) wide; add ¼in (5mm) to length for each larger size. Draw center front line and grain line along center of rectangle. Measurements include ⅝in (1.5cm) seam allowance on all edges.

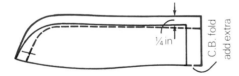

19 To make the collar pattern, measure the neck seamline from the center back to shoulder seamline and from shoulder seamline to the front button extension foldline. Add these two measurements together to get half the neckline measurement.
20 Measure along the neck seamline of the shirt collar from the front edge to the center back. Subtract this amount from the neckline measurement and add the difference between them to the center back edge of the collar. For example, if the neckline is 10in (25cm) and the collar seamline 9in (23cm) add 1in (2.5cm) to center back edge of collar.
21 Make the collar ¼in (6mm) deeper and exaggerate the curve at front edge. This should be drawn freehand. The finished width of the collar should be approximately 1¾in (4.5cm).

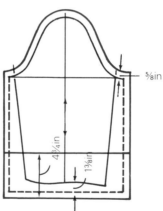

24 To lengthen sleeve, add 1⅜in (3.5cm) to the lower edge and draw a straight line across. Draw the underarm seamlines straight down to the lower edge. Add ⅝in (1.5cm) seam allowance to all edges of sleeve. Draw a line across the sleeve pattern 4¾in (12cm) up from lower edge to separate the two halves of the lining. Cut through this line and add ⅝in (1.5cm) seam allowance to each piece.

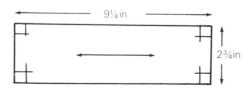

25 To make front sleeve strap pattern, draw a rectangle 9¼ × 2¾in (23.5 × 7cm)

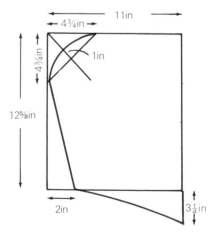

29 To make the hood pattern, draw a rectangle 11in (28cm) wide by 12⅝in (32cm) long. Drop lower right-hand edge 3¼in (8cm) to make front of hood. Take 2in (5cm) from lower left-hand edge.

This will be the back of the hood. To curve the crown, measure along both edges of rectangle from left-hand top corner 4¾in (12cm). Connect these two points with a flexible curve, moving the curve out 1in (2.5cm) at center from straight line which connects the two.

30 Continue the center back line along to the lower edge and onto the front edge as shown, making the last line slightly concave.

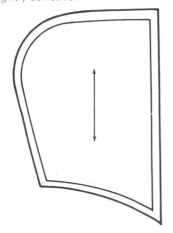

31 Add ⅝in (1.5cm) seam allowances to all edges of hood. Mark the grain line parallel to the front edge, which is the longest straight line.

Lining and detachable lining

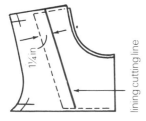

1 To make the front yoke lining pattern, fold the front facing in place. Working from the right side of the pattern piece, draw the lining cutting line 1¼in (3cm) away from and parallel to the outer cutting line of the facing.

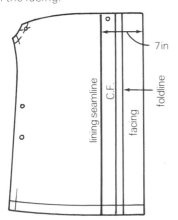

2 To make front lining pattern, measure in 7in (18cm) from front facing cutting line

and draw lining cutting line from the top to the hem edge, keeping it parallel to center front. Cut 6in (15cm) off hem length for detachable lining.

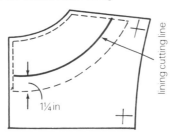

3 To make the back yoke lining pattern, lay the back neck facing underneath the back yoke. Working from the right side of the yoke pattern, measure in 1¼in (3cm) from the outer edge of the facing and draw the lining cutting line from the center back to the shoulder, keeping the line parallel to the facing edge.

4 To make the back lining pattern, fold the back pleat in place on the back pattern, and cut the lining pattern from this, following all pattern and cutting lines. Cut detachable lining 6in (15cm) shorter at hem.

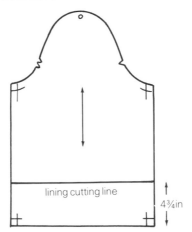

5 To make the sleeve lining pattern, draw a line across sleeve pattern 4¾in (12cm) up from lower edge to separate the two halves of lining. Cut through this line and add ⅝in (1.5cm) seam allowances to each piece on this edge.

Notes for sleeve and sleeve lining adaptations

The lower part of the sleeve is lined in contrasting fabric and the upper part in plain lining. To make the sleeve lining from one fabric only, omit the seam in the pattern adaptation. To determine the width adjustment of the sleeve for sizes larger than size 10, measure along the armhole seamlines of the front yoke and front and the back yoke and back. Add these two measurements together. Measure around the sleeve cap seamline after raising the sleeve cap as explained. The difference between this measurement

and the last is added to the horizontal line of the sleeve at underarm (equal amounts on each side). So, if front yoke and armhole seamline measure 8⅝in (22cm) and back yoke and armhole seamline measure 8¼in (21cm), the total armhole measurement is 16⅞in (43cm). If sleeve seamline is 14⅛in (36cm), the difference is 2¾in (7cm). Therefore 1⅜in (3.5cm) is added to each side of armhole on horizontal line. Directions for assembling the raincoat are given on page 83.

Sewing/COURSE 67

*Detachable hood
*Detachable lining
*Pattern for a hooded
  raincoat (2):
  directions for making

Detachable hood

A detachable hood is easy to make and lends itself to many designs. The obvious choice is to put it on a jacket or coat, as on the raincoat shown on page 84, but it could also look great on a dress, sweater or blouse, made in a suitable fabric.

The pattern for the hood is on page 80. Check that the lower edge of the hood fits neatly around the shoulders before cutting out.

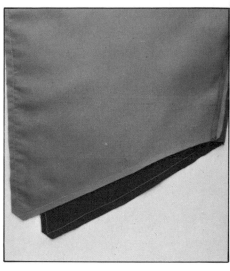

1 With right sides together, baste and stitch the center back seam of hood and hood lining. Trim the seam allowances to $\frac{3}{8}$in (1cm) and press the seam open.

2 With right sides together, slip the lining over the hood and baste both pieces together around front and neck edges. Stitch around these edges, leaving 4in (10cm) open at back neck to turn hood right side out. Trim seam allowances and cut across the front corners.

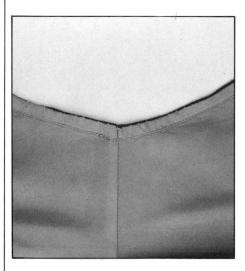

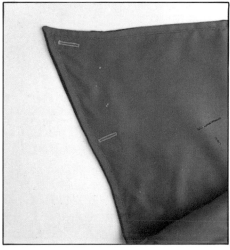

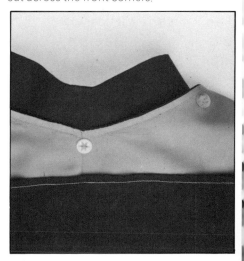

3 Turn hood right side out through the opening and baste around stitched edges. At the opening turn under the seam allowances and slip stitch the two edges together. Press. To prevent the lining from slipping or rolling, topstitch around the front and neck edges, stitching $\frac{1}{4}$in (5mm) in from these edges. Press.

4 Work vertical buttonholes at the neck edge of the hood: one at the center back, one at each shoulder point and one at each front edge. Start the buttonholes close to the stitching and make them $\frac{1}{8}$in (3mm) longer than the diameter of the button.

5 Sew buttons to the raincoat just below the neck seamline to correspond with the buttonholes on the hood. The hood can be fastened from either side: if the right side of the hood is facing the right side of the coat it will lie flatter.

Detachable lining

A detachable lining is a simple way of adding warmth to a light raincoat. Worn on its own, it makes a simple vest for fall or spring.

The lining made here is a simple quilted lining, which can be attached to the main garment with buttons or snaps. The main sections are joined before the fabric is quilted, and then the edges are bound with matching or contrasting fabric.

For the raincoat on page 84, we used a tartan plaid fabric to match the lining of the detachable hood and other details. The backing fabric is plain, to match the lining of the raincoat.

The detachable lining could also be made in a fleecy fabric and simply bound around the edges.

1 After joining back and fronts and quilting, trim all seams and press them open. Stitch the seam allowances down by machine-stitching $\frac{1}{4}$in (6mm) away from the seamline on each side.

2 Trim off lower hem to the length required. Using a wide bias binding or self-fabric bias strip, cut $\frac{3}{4}$in (2cm) wider than usual, bind the neck, front, hem and armhole edges of the lining.

3 Mark vertical buttonholes all around the neck and front edges near the binding seamline. The number will vary according to size of button and length of lining. There should be buttonholes at center back and shoulder points. Buttons will be sewn to raincoat facing just above lining seam to correspond. If using snaps, sew the two halves to the lining binding and the garment placing them at 4in (10cm) intervals.

Hooded raincoat (2)

Here the directions continue for making the hooded raincoat begun on page 78. This version has a detachable lining made to match the lined hood.

Directions for making

Suggested fabrics
Rainproof or showerproof fabrics such as laminated cotton and blends, light to medium-weight cotton, pinwale corduroy, velvet and velveteen, gabardine and lamé. Some fabrics can be shower-proofed after the garment has been completed. Linings: synthetics or lightweight cotton.
Note: Here we have made two versions of the raincoat—for the one shown on page 78, we used 45in (115cm)-wide silver lamé lined throughout with 45in (115cm)-wide plain lining. For the one shown on page 84, we used 45in (115cm)-wide velveteen, partly lined with 45in (115cm)-wide plain lining, with 45in (115cm)-wide contrasting lining for hood, facings and details. This version has a quilted detachable lining attached with buttons or snaps. Both versions have a lined, button-on hood.

Materials
Raincoat fabric
    45in (115cm)-wide fabric with or
        without nap:
        Size 10: 4$\frac{1}{2}$yd (4.1m)
        Sizes 12, 14: 4$\frac{5}{8}$yd (4.2m)
        Sizes 16-20: 4$\frac{7}{8}$yd (4.4m)
Lining—Versions 1 and 2
    45in (115cm)-wide fabric with or
        without nap:
        Sizes 10, 12: 4$\frac{3}{8}$yd (3.9m)
        Sizes 14, 16: 4$\frac{3}{8}$yd (4m)
        Sizes 18, 20: 4$\frac{1}{2}$yd (4.1m)
    45in (115cm)-wide contrasting
        fabric with or without nap: For all
        sizes: 1$\frac{1}{8}$yd (1m)

Detachable lining—optional
    45in (115cm)-wide fabric with or
        without nap:
        For all sizes: 2$\frac{7}{8}$yd (2.6m)

45in (115cm)-wide batting and
    backing: For all sizes: 2$\frac{7}{8}$yd (2.6m)
    of each—optional (for quilted
    version only)
Snap fasteners or $\frac{3}{8}$in (1cm)-diameter
    buttons
2 cards wide bias binding—optional

Interfacing
    36in (90cm)-wide sew-in:
        For all sizes: 1$\frac{1}{4}$yd (1.1m)

Matching thread
Two 1$\frac{1}{8}$in (3cm)-wide buckles
Shoulder pads
Small eyelets (to fit buckle
    prong)
Eight $\frac{1}{2}$in (1.2cm)-diameter buttons
    for front fastening
Five $\frac{3}{8}$in (1cm)-diameter buttons
    for hood

Simon Butcher

Stefano Massimo

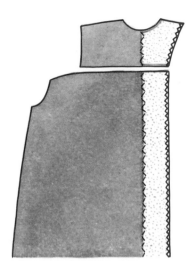

1 Cut out, following layouts and notes below. Baste interfacing to the wrong side of the front facings and front yoke facings. Catch-stitch interfacing to foldlines and finish facing edges.

2 Fold, baste and stitch center back pleat in place. Press pleat carefully from the right side.

3 Run two rows of gathering stitches across the top edge of the fronts and back. The first row is ¾in (2cm) below the edge and the second row ¼in (5mm) below the first.

Key to adapted pattern pieces
For both versions

A Back yoke	Cut 1 on fold
B Back	Cut 1 on fold
C Back neck facing	Cut 1 on fold
D Front yoke and facing	Cut 2
E Front	Cut 2
F Front fly facing	Cut 2
G Collar	Cut 2 on fold
H Sleeve	Cut 2
I Front sleeve strap	Cut 2
J Back sleeve strap	Cut 2
K Hood	Cut 2

Lining

M Back yoke	Cut 1 on fold
N Back	Cut 1 on fold
O Front yoke	Cut 2
P Front	Cut 2
Q Sleeve and sleeve facing	Cut 2

R Hood	Cut 2
S Pocket	Cut 2

Detachable lining

M Back yoke	Cut 1 on fold
N Back	Cut 1 on fold
O Front yoke	Cut 2
P Front	Cut 2

Interfacing: use pieces D, E, C, G cut to shape as directed.

Note: Cut back and front detachable linings 6in (15cm) shorter than linings and trim off 3in (8cm) from pattern at center front and center back (not yoke patterns). The main parts will be eased, not gathered, onto yokes to reduce bulkiness if using quilted or thick pile fabrics. When cutting fabric for quilted sections, cut ¾in (2cm) bigger all around to allow for reduction after quilting. Trim to pattern size after quilting.

The front and back pieces of the outer garment are gathered onto the yokes and the gathering stitches remain as a detail. When stitching the gathering rows, use a slightly smaller stitch than normally used for gathering.

36in-wide fabric
INTERFACING
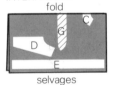

45in-wide fabric, with or without nap
RAINCOAT

45in-wide fabric, with or without nap
LINING
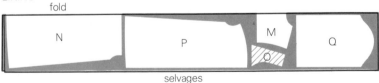

45in-wide fabric, with or without nap
CONTRAST LINING
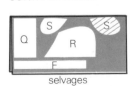

45in-wide fabric, with or without nap
DETACHABLE LINING
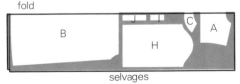

Brian Mayor

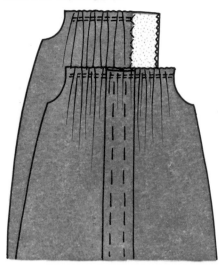

4 Pull the gathering threads up carefully until each piece fits the yoke. Spread the gathers evenly across each piece and then tie off the threads on the wrong side.

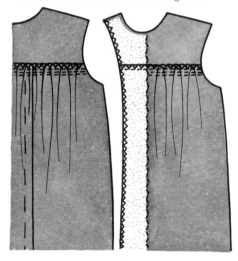

5 With right sides together, baste and stitch the front yokes to the fronts and the back yoke to the back, taking a ⅝in (1.5cm) seam allowance. Press the seam upward and finish the edges together.

6 With right sides together, baste and stitch the shoulder seams of the yokes and neck facings. Press seams open.

7 Fold the front facings to the inside along the foldline and baste the facing along the folded edge and around the neck edge. Press, Catch-stitch the facings to the shoulder seams.

8 Mark two vertical buttonholes ⅝in (1.5cm) long on the right front yoke on the center front line. The first is ½in (1.2cm) from the neck edge and the second ½in (1.2cm) up from the yoke line.
9 Mark five more buttonholes along the center front line on the right front. The first is 2¾in (7cm) below yoke seamline and the other four at 3½in (9cm) intervals. Measure from the center of each buttonhole each time. Work buttonholes by hand or by machine.

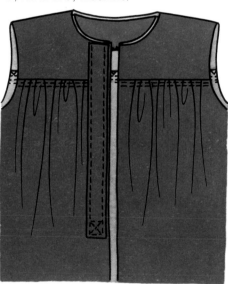

10 Make a false fly facing, using a contrasting fabric for the inner facing, as shown on page 77. Add a row of topstitching down the outer edge of the facing. Stitch the fly facing to the right front as shown. Press.

11 Baste the interfacing to the wrong side of one collar piece. With right sides together, baste and stitch the two collar pieces together, leaving neck edge open. Trim interfacing close to stitching and trim seam allowance. Turn collar right side out and baste close to the stitched edge. Press.

12 Pin the interfaced edge of the collar to the right side of the neck edge and baste in place, matching center backs and front edges. Stitch the seam. Clip and grade the seam allowances, trimming the interfacing close to the stitching. Press the seam allowance toward the collar.

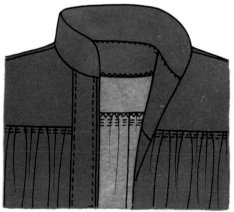

13 On the inside, turn under the seam allowance of the inner collar and slip stitch to the stitching line, enclosing all raw edges. Topstitch ¼in (6mm) in from the upper edge of the collar. Press.

Terry Evans

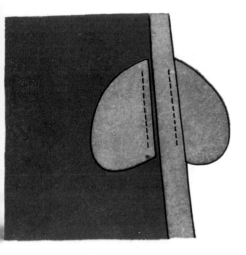

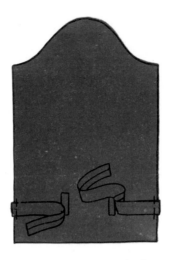

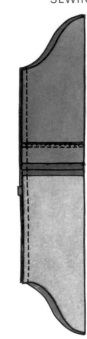

14 With right sides together, baste and stitch each pocket piece to the back and front side seams in positions marked on the pattern. Press seam allowances toward the pocket pieces.

18 Baste the longer strap to the front edge of the sleeve and the shorter strap to the back edge, matching raw edges. The lower edge of each strap should be 3½in (9cm) up from lower edge of sleeve.
19 Make two fabric carriers for each sleeve to slip the straps through. Sew each carrier to the right side of the sleeve, positioning them 4in (10cm) in from the side edges of the sleeve.

22 Open sleeve sections out, and with right sides together, baste and stitch the underarm seam of sleeve and sleeve lining. Press seam open. Be sure not to catch the sleeve straps when stitching.

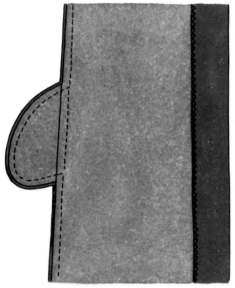

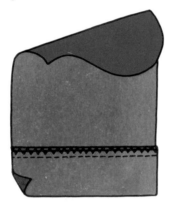

15 With right sides together, baste and stitch the side seams. Press seams open. Complete pockets as shown in Volume 5, page 72.

20 With right sides together, baste and stitch the lower part of the sleeve lining (contrast piece) to the upper part of the sleeve lining. Press seam allowances upward and finish together.

23 With wrong sides together, bring the lining up inside the sleeve and baste around the lower edge. Press. Topstitch ¼in (6mm) in from this edge.

16 Make sleeve straps by folding each strap in half lengthwise with right sides together. Stitch along the edge, taking a ⅝in (1.5cm) seam. Trim seam to ¼in (6mm) and press open with the seamline in the center of each strap.

17 Stitch across one short end, taking a ⅝in (1.5cm) seam. Trim seam, clip corners and turn right side out. Press.

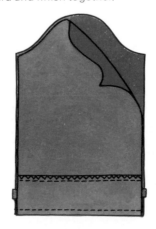

21 With right sides together, baste and stitch the sleeve lining to the lower edge of the sleeve. Press seam allowances toward the sleeve.

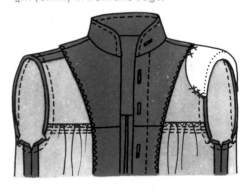

24 With right sides together and seams and shoulder points matching, pin and baste the sleeve into armhole. Stitch seam with sleeve side up. Trim seam and clip curves. Press seam allowances toward sleeve and finish them together. Sew the shoulder pads in place as directed in Volume 9, page 61.

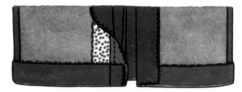

25 At the lower edge of the raincoat, turn the front facing outward and turn up the 2in (5cm) hem allowance. Sew hem in place with invisible hemming stitch. Remove basting stitches and press. Turn the front facing back to the inside and hem to the hem allowance. Press.

Lining and finishing

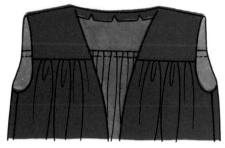

1 Gather the fronts onto the front yokes and the back onto the back yoke using the ordinary gathering method. Press seam upward and finish edges together.
2 With right sides together, baste and stitch the shoulder seams and side seams. Press all seams open. Turn under a $\frac{5}{8}$in (1.5cm) seam allowance around the neck edge, clipping the seam allowance to enable the seam to lie flat. Press flat.

3 With wrong sides together and shoulder and side seams matching, pin the lining into the raincoat around armhole, neck and front edges, overlapping the facing by $\frac{5}{8}$in (1.5cm). Baste and slip stitch lining to the facings to within 6in (15cm) of the lower edge and press.
4 At the lower edge, trim 1in (2.5cm) off lining all around. Turn up a $1\frac{3}{8}$in (3.5cm) hem allowance and baste close to folded edge. Press. Machine-stitch lining over basting, remove basting and finish slip stitching lining to facings. The lining length allows ease of movement.
5 Press the lining down, covering the edge of the garment hem. Sew the lining to the armhole seam allowance using back stitch.

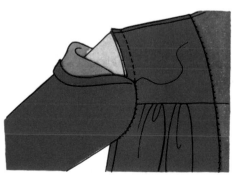

6 Bring the sleeve lining up over the armhole seam allowance. Turn in the

lining seam allowance and slip stitch it to the seamline. Press.

7 Sew the buckles to back sleeve straps and make eyelets to correspond in the front sleeve straps. Make detachable hood as shown on page 82, using contrasting lining. Sew buttons for hood in appropriate positions below neck seamline. Sew buttons to left yoke and front underneath buttonholes. Make detachable lining as shown on page 83.

Needlework / COURSE 18

*Machine embroidery—
 special effects
*Satin stitch effects
*Transferring a design—
 perforation method
*A machine-embroidered
 panel

Machine embroidery—special effects

In ordinary machine stitching it's important to keep the upper and lower tensions even, so that the threads lock in the center of the fabric. In free machine embroidery, however, some of the most attractive effects are created by altering the tensions —especially by loosening the lower and tightening the upper, thus bringing the bobbin thread to the surface so that it covers the top thread partially or completely.

By using different colors in the needle and bobbin you can produce interesting two-color effects. The range of possibilities is extended even further by using a variety of threads in the bobbin. Embroidery threads, such as pearl cotton and Persian yarn, and fine knitting yarns, including metallic yarns, are some of the threads that can be used.

Whip stitch To produce this corded effect, first thread the machine needle with a strong sewing thread, such as size 40, and wind the bobbin with fine machine embroidery thread (size 50). Set the upper tension to nearly maximum and the lower to about half the usual tension. Run the machine fast and move the frame slowly and smoothly, so that the bobbin thread completely covers the top one.

For an interesting two-color effect use different-colored threads in the needle and bobbin and move the hoop at different speeds. In this sample a yellow thread has been used in the needle, a white one in the bobbin. Where the yellow shows, the frame was moved quickly, so that the stitches are longer and the bobbin thread loops spaced apart; where only the white shows, the hoop was moved slowly.

Here again, a yellow thread was used in the needle, a white one in the bobbin. The machine was run fast and the frame moved slowly, as for whip stitch, but a relatively loose top tension has caused small loops of yellow to break out sideways, forming a textured line.

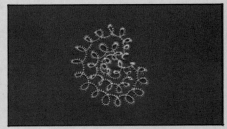

Feather stitch is produced by setting the upper tension at its tightest, the lower at its loosest, and stitching in a spiral. This draws long loops of bobbin thread to the surface.

Cable stitch An interesting effect is produced by using a textured thread in the bobbin and placing the fabric right side down. Loosening the lower tension produces a crinkly effect, as in the lines worked in coton à broder and Persian yarn.

Satin stitch effects

Satin stitch (that is, close zig-zag) is most often used in lines, but it can also be used effectively in various other ways. By stitching in the same place a number of times you can build up shiny little blobs that provide an interesting contrast with surrounding lines of stitches. Use a wide stitch and hold the frame still. After working a blob, make one straight stitch to the position of the next one; don't cut the thread, as this may cause unraveling.

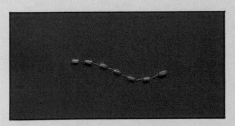

These little satin stitch blobs add textural interest to an area of straight running stitch.

For satin stitch stars work several narrow blobs radiating from a central hole. If the needle stops on the outside, turn the wheel to bring it to the center.

Frederick Mancini

Transferring a design—perforation method

1 Make a tracing of the design. Then place it wrong side up on a flat, padded surface. Using a large needle, prick holes along the lines of the design, placing them $\frac{1}{4}$in (5mm) or less apart. Or, if you prefer, prick holes by machine with an unthreaded needle and the longest stitch.

2 Place the tracing right side up on the fabric and pin or weight it in place. Using a rolled-up piece of felt, or absorbent cotton, rub pounce (a powder made for this purpose) or talcum powder through the holes. Rub in a circular motion.

3 Carefully remove the tracing. Using a fine paintbrush and poster paint matching the fabric, paint over the outlines formed by the dots of powder, making the line as thin as possible. Blow away or shake off the excess powder. (Use this method for complex designs or those to be transferred more than once.)

Petal smooth

The translucent petals of this blossom are created by overlapping lines of machine running stitch and whip stitch. You can make the motif any size you like and use it for a panel, as shown here, or on a pillow cover or scarf.

Materials
1yd (1m) of closely-woven cotton or cotton-synthetic fabric in a medium to dark color
Machine embroidery thread, size 50, in five colors: A, B, C (contrasting with the fabric, such as the white, cream and yellow used here), D and E (medium and light shades harmonizing with the fabric); if machine embroidery thread is not available use the finest available sewing thread.
Cotton sewing thread, size 40, in colors A, B and C
Embroidery hoop about 10in (25cm) in diameter
Paper for enlarging the design; ruler
2 sheets of tracing paper
Pounce or talcum powder and cotton
Poster paint matching fabric and fine paintbrush
Button thread
Piece of particleboard 14×15in (36×38cm) (or desired size)

1 Cut a piece of fabric 2in (5cm) larger all around than the piece of particleboard.
2 Using the method described in Volume 4, page 76; enlarge the flower design to the desired size. The embroidery shown in the photograph is about 12in (30cm) in diameter; each square on the pattern corresponds to 1sq. in (2.5sq. cm) on the embroidery.
3 Make two tracings of the flower: one of the broken lines and one of the solid lines and small circles.
Note: Before proceeding with the complete embroidery you should practice working parts of the design on spare fabric.
4 Using the perforation method described above, transfer the broken line petals of the first tracing to the fabric. Join

the powder dots with a fine line of poster paint. You may also want to paint a line down the center of each petal as an additional guide.

5 Frame the fabric as shown in Volume 11, page 88, making sure that the fabric is very taut.

6 Prepare the machine for embroidery as described in Volume 11, page 88. Thread the needle and wind the bobbin with machine embroidery thread in color A, C or D. Adjust the tension and stitch length to produce a short running stitch.

7 Now work the running stitch petals, following the key on the right for placement of colors. Work all the petals within the hoop (in any color order), then re-frame the fabric for the adjacent group of petals. Start each petal by working around the marked outline, from the flower center to the point and back again. At the point, reverse the direction of the hoop so that you are stitching backward—rather than pivoting the fabric around the needle. Now fill in the petal with more lines of stitching, placing them as close together as possible and working in a continuous line. The turning points should follow each other in a smoothly curved line down the center of the petal. There should be only a slight build-up of thread at these points.

8 Again using the powder, transfer the solid line petals from the second tracing onto the fabric. Follow the original design to get the placement correct.

9 Thread the machine needle with ordinary sewing thread in color A, B or C and wind the bobbin with machine embroidery thread in the same color. Adjust the upper and lower tension to produce a smooth whip stitch, as described on page 89. Work the remaining petals, following the key for color placement.

10 Draw the thread ends to the wrong side and cut them off, leaving ½in (1.2cm) ends.

11 On the second tracing perforate the center of each satin stitch star and also the line joining the petals. (If you prefer you can work this part of the design freehand, using your eye as a guide.) Transfer the motifs to the fabric as before.

12 Set the machine to a wide satin stitch. Using color D, work the 7 stars in the center, as shown on page 89. Using color E, work the rest of the stars.

13 Using color A, work two lines of whip stitch joining the petals.

14 Using color D and running stitch, work circles around the stars, and fill in the areas between stars and whip stitch lines with a very small scribbling movement. Draw the ends to the wrong side and trim them. Press the embroidery on the wrong side.

15 Turn under the edge of the fabric ¾in (2cm) and machine stitch twice along each edge, close to the fold.

16 Thread a needle with button thread,

Color key

A	3, 5, 6, 9, 15, 17, 20, 23, 27, 30
B	7, 13, 22, 28
C	2, 4, 10, 11, 16, 18, 21, 24, 25, 29
D	1, 8, 12, 14, 19, 26

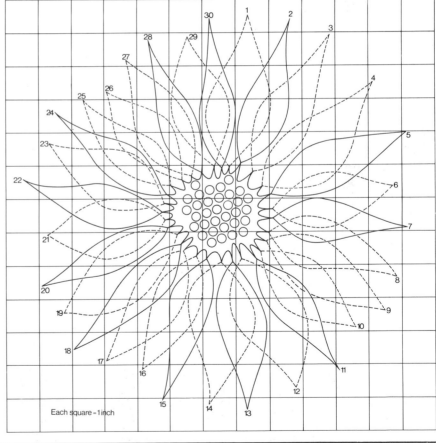

Each square = 1 inch

but do not cut off the end. Place the embroidery face down on a flat surface and lay the board on top of it. Fold the upper and lower fabric edges over the board and, starting at the upper left-hand corner, take the needle through each edge alternately, placing the stitches about ½in (1.2cm) apart. When you reach the end, cut off the thread, pull it tightly and anchor it at both ends. Repeat with the remaining two edges of the fabric.

17 Have the embroidery framed, preferably without glass.

CROCHET

Strawberry sweater

We've added mouth-watering strawberry motifs to this delectable sweater to remind you of warm summer days.

Sizes
To fit 32[34:36]in (83[87:92]cm) bust.
Length, 21[21½:22¼]in (53[54.5:56.5] cm).
Sleeve, 18¼[18¾:19¼]in (45[47:48]cm).
Note Directions for larger sizes are in brackets []; if there is only one set of figures it applies to all sizes.

Materials
15[17:17]oz (400[450:450]g) of a knitting worsted in main color (A)
1oz (25g) each in 2 contrasting colors (B and C)
Sizes F and H (4.00 and 5.00mm) crochet hooks

Gauge
16dc and 7 rows to 4in (10cm) worked on size H (5.00mm) hook.

Right side
*Using size F (4.00mm) hook and A make 32[36:40] ch for cuff edge.
Base row 1dc into 4th ch from hook, 1dc into each ch to end. Turn. 30[34:38]dc.

Ribbing row 2ch, *work around next dc by working yo, insert hook from front to back between next 2dc, around dc at left and through work from back to front, draw yarn through and complete dc in usual way – called double around front or dc around Ft –, work around next dc by working yo, insert hook from back to front between next 2dc, around dc at left and through work from front to back, draw yarn through and complete dc in usual way – called double around back or dc around Bk –, rep from * to end. Turn.
Rep ribbing row 6 times more.
Inc row 3ch to count as first dc, 1dc into first dc, *1dc into next dc, 2dc into next dc, rep from * to end, 1dc into turning ch. Turn. 45[51:57]dc.
Change to size H (5.00mm) hook.
Next row 3ch to count as first dc, 1dc into each dc to end. Turn.
Rep last row 12[13:14] times more.
Shape sleeve
Next row 3ch, 2dc into first dc, 1dc into each dc to within last dc, 3dc into last dc. Turn.

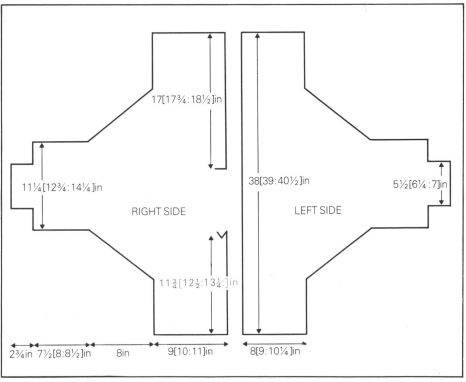

17[17¾:18½]in

11¼[12¾:14¼]in

RIGHT SIDE

11¾[12½:13¼]in

38[39:40½]in

LEFT SIDE

5½[6¼:7]in

2¾in 7½[8:8½]in 8in 9[10:11]in 8[9:10¼]in

Brian Mayor

Rep last row 11 times more. 93[99:105] dc. Beg patt.

1st row (WS) 3ch, 2dc into first dc, 1dc into each of next 45[48:51] dc joining in B on last dc, with B work 5dc all into next dc for base of first strawberry, cut off B, work 1dc into each dc to within last dc, 3dc into last dc. Turn.

2nd row 3ch, 2dc into first dc, 1dc into each dc to within base of strawberry joining in C on last dc, with C work 1dc into next dc, now leaving last loop of each on hook work 1dc into each of next 4dc, wind A around hook and draw through all loops on hook, cut off C, 1dc into each dc to within last dc, 3dc into last dc. Fasten off and turn.

Next row With A make 30ch, with WS facing rejoin to sleeve by working 3dc into first dc; work to within 5dc of strawberry in previous row, 1 strawberry base into next st, 1dc into each of next 9dc, 1 strawberry base into next st; cont in patt to within last dc, 3dc into last dc, work 32ch. Turn.

Next row 1dc into 4th ch from hook, 1dc into each ch, patt across sleeve, completing strawberries as position is reached; 1dc into each ch to end. Turn. Cont to work strawberry motifs, positioning them so that 9dc are worked between each strawberry on every row; add 1 strawberry at each end every time, alternating positions of strawberries as set. Carry yarn not in use along top of preceding row and work over it in new color. Cut off color at the end of the row when color is no longer required. Work 13[15:17] rows without shaping.*

Shape for V

Next row Patt until this row measures 11¾[12½:13¼]in (30[32:34]cm), work next 4dc tog, turn.

Next row 3ch, 3dc into first dc, patt to end. Fasten off.

Shape for back neck

With WS facing skip next 8¾[8¼:8¼]in (22[21:21]cm) at center neck, join A to next st, 3ch, patt to end. Turn. Patt 1 row. Fasten off.

Left side

Work as right side from * to *. Fasten off.

To finish

Join front and back seams, then join side and underarm seams.

Waistband

With RS facing and using size F (4.00mm) hook join A to one side seam on lower edge and work an even number of sc evenly around lower edge, sl st into first sc.

Next round 3ch, 1dc into each sc to end, sl st into top of 3ch.

1st ribbing round 2ch, *1dc around Ft, 1dc around Bk, rep from * all around, sl st into top of 2ch.

2nd ribbing round 2ch, *1dc around Bk, 1dc around Ft, rep from * all around, sl st into top of 2ch.

Rep last 2 rounds once more, then work the first ribbing round again. Fasten off.

Neck edging

With RS of work facing and using size F (4.00mm) hook join on A and work a row of sc evenly all around neck edge. Fasten off. Work 1 round in C and 1 round in B. Fasten off.

Snug for sleeping

Stripes and flowers in pretty pastels decorate this blanket and sleeping bag.

Sizes
Blanket 34×26in (88×68cm).
Sleeping bag to fit up to six months.
Length, 25in (63cm).
Sleeve seam, 4¾in (12cm).

Materials
15oz (420g) of a sport yarn in white
7oz (180g) in blue
6oz (140g) in green
5oz (120g) in yellow
4oz (100g) in pink
Sizes E and F (3.50 and 4.00mm)
crochet hooks
24in (61cm) open-ended zipper
4 buttons

Gauge
Blanket 1 motif measures 4¾in (12cm)
square worked on size F (4.00mm) hook.
Sleeping bag 20dc and 11 rows to 4in
(10cm) worked on size E (3.50mm) hook.

Blanket

First strip
Motif
Using size F (4.00mm) hook and
white, make 6ch. Join with a sl st into
first ch to form a ring.
1st round Work 16sc into ring. Join with
a sl st into first sc.
2nd round 6ch, *skip 1sc, 1dc into next
sc, 3ch, rep from * 6 times.
Join with a sl st to 3rd of first 6ch.
Fasten off white. 8sps.
3rd round Join blue with a sl st to any sp,
(1sc, 1hdc, 3dc, 1hdc, 1sc) all into same
3ch sp, *(1sc, 1hdc, 3dc, 1hdc, 1sc) all
into next 3ch sp, rep from * 6 times. Join
with a sl st to first sc. 8 petals.
4th round *5ch, 1sc around stem of next
dc on 2nd row, keeping to back of work,
rep from * 7 times more, catching up base
of first 5ch of round on last sc to bring it
in line with other 5ch loops.
5th round Into each 5ch loop work (1sc,
1hdc, 5dc, 1hdc, 1sc). Join with a sl st to
first sc.
6th round *5ch, 1sc around next sc of 4th
round, keeping the 5ch to back of work as
on 4th round, rep from * 7 times, ending
as for 4th round. Cut off blue.
7th round Join white with a sl st to any
5ch loop, 3ch, 5dc into same loop, *3ch,
6dc into next 5ch loop, 6dc into next 5ch
loop, rep from * twice more, 3ch, 6dc
into next 5ch loop. Join with a sl st to 3rd
of first 3ch. 4 sets of 12dc separated with
corner sp of 3ch.
8th round 3ch, 1dc into each of next 5dc,
*(2dc, 2ch, 2dc) in corner sp, 1dc in each
of next 12dc, rep from * twice more, (2dc,
2ch, 2dc) in next corner sp, 1dc in each
of last 6dc. Join with a sl st to top of first
3ch.
9th round 3ch, 1dc into each of next 7dc,
*(2dc, 2ch, 2dc) in corner sp, 1dc into
each of next 16dc, rep from * twice more,
(2dc, 2ch, 2dc) in corner sp, 1dc in each

of last 8dc. Join with a sl st into top of
first 3ch. Fasten off.
Make 5 more motifs in the same way,
using blue for the petals of one more
motif, pink for the petals of two motifs,
then one green and one yellow.
Join motifs into a strip. Place WS of 2
motifs tog and using pink, work a row
of sc across one edge (working through
both thicknesses). Join in this order:
blue to pink; green to blue; yellow to
green; blue to yellow; pink to blue.
Edging of strip
1st row Using white and with RS facing,
work along long edge of strip, sl st into
corner sp of first motif, 3ch, *work 1dc
into each of next 20dc, 1dc into next
corner sp, 1dc into corner sp of next
motif, rep from * along all 6 motifs,
ending with 1dc in corner sp of last motif.
Turn. 132sts.
2nd row Using pink, 3ch, skip first dc,
1dc into each dc, ending with 1dc into top
of 3ch. Turn.
3rd row Using green, 3ch, skip first dc,
*5dc in next dc, drop loop on hook, insert
hook into first of these 5dc from front to
back and draw dropped loop through —
bobble made, 1dc into each of next 2dc,
rep from * ending with 1 bobble, 1dc
into top of 3ch. Turn.
4th row Using pink, 3ch, skip first dc,
1dc into each st to end. 132sts.
5th row Using white, 3ch, skip first dc,
1dc into each dc, ending with 1dc into
top of 3ch. Turn.
6th row As 5th.
7th row Using yellow, as 3rd.
8th row Using white, as 6th.
9th row As 8th.
10th row Using blue, as 6th.
11th row As 10th. Fasten off.
Turn work and rep last 11 rows.
along other long edge of strip.
Second strip
Work as for first strip.
Join strips tog.
Place RS tog and using blue, work along
one long side, working 1sc into each st
through both thicknesses.
Top and lower edging
With RS facing, join blue to first row end
of strip edging along short edge of work,
3ch, *(2dc into next row end, 1dc into
next row end) to corner sp of motif, 1dc
into corner sp, 1dc into each of 20dc on
motif, 1dc into next corner sp, rep from *
once more, ending with (1dc into next
row end, 2dc into next row end) to last
row end, 1dc into last row end. Turn.
108sts.
Next row Using blue, 3ch, skip first dc,
1dc into each dc, ending with 1dc into
top of 3ch. Fasten off.
Make a similar edging along other
short edge.
Picot edging
With RS facing, join blue to first st on
short edge of work, **work *1sc into each
of next 3sts, 5ch, sl st into sc just worked

(picot) *, rep from * to * to corner, turn
corner, work 2sc in row end, 1sc in next
row end, 5ch, sl st into last sc, then work
from * to * to next corner, working 3sc
into 2 row ends before corner, **, rep
from ** to ** for other 2 sides of blanket.
Join with a sl st to first sc.
Fasten off.

Sleeping bag

Using size E (3.50mm) hook throughout,
make 6 motifs as for blanket — 2 in blue,
2 in yellow, 1 in pink and 1 in green, but
work a 10th round so that there are 20dc
between corners.

Back
With RS facing and using pink, join 1
blue and 1 yellow motif tog with sc in
same way as blanket. With RS facing and
using white, work across breadth of 2
motifs as foll: rejoin yarn to first corner
sp on blue motif, 3ch, 1dc into each dc
across this motif, 1dc into corner sp on
this motif, 1dc into corner sp on yellow
motif, 1dc into each dc of this motif, 1dc
into corner sp. 52sts. Turn.
Next row Using pink, 3ch, skip first dc, 1dc
into each st, ending with 1dc into top of
3ch. Turn.
Next row Using green, work a row of
bobbles as for blanket. Turn.
Next row Using pink, 3ch, skip first st,
1dc into each st, ending with 1dc into top
of 3ch. Turn.
Cont working in dc and stripe sequence
as foll: 2 rows white, 1 row yellow
bobbles, 2 rows white, 1 row each of
blue, white, pink, white, green, white,
yellow, 7 rows white, 1 row each yellow,
white, green, white, pink, white, blue, 2
rows white, 1 row yellow bobbles, 2 rows
white, 1 row pink, 1 row green bobbles,
1 row pink, 7 rows white, 1 row each
blue, white, pink, white, green, white,
yellow, white.
Join tog 1 blue and 1 yellow motif with
pink sc on RS of work. Using pink sc in
same way, join 2 motifs to last row of
back.
Shoulders
With RS facing and using blue, work
52dc across unworked edge of first 2
motifs of back. Turn.
Work 2 rows in dc.
Fasten off.

Left front
Along one edge of pink motif work 26dc
in white.
Now work as back from first row of dc
in pink to end, excluding addition of two
motifs on lower edge.
Shoulder
With RS facing, join blue to right-hand
corner of pink motif, 3ch, 1dc into each of
next 17dc. Turn.
Work 2 rows in dc.
Fasten off.

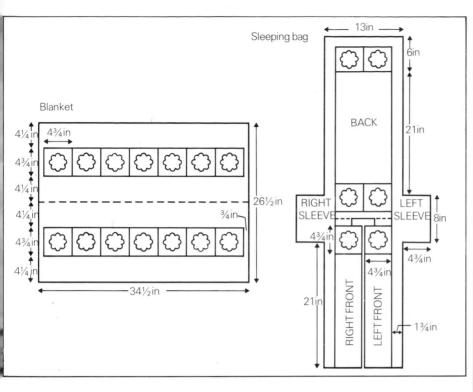

Blanket

4¼ in · 4¾ in · 4¾ in · 4¼ in · 4¼ in · 4¾ in · 4¼ in

26½ in · ¾ in

34½ in

Sleeping bag

13in · 6in

BACK

21in

RIGHT SLEEVE · LEFT SLEEVE · 8in

4¾in · 4¾in

21in

RIGHT FRONT · LEFT FRONT

4¾in · 1¾in

Right front
Work as left, but use green motif.

Shoulder
With RS facing skip corner sp and first 2dc of green motif, rejoin blue to next dc, 3ch, 1dc into each dc to end and 1dc into corner sp. Turn.
Work 2 rows in dc. Fasten off. Join shoulder seams.

Side edges and sleeves
With RS facing join blue to first row end on lower edge of left front.
1st row 3ch, 1dc into same place as joining, *1dc into next row end 2dc into next row end *, rep from * to * along side of left front to motif, 1dc into each dc of motif, then rep from * to * once more across shoulders, 1dc into each dc of motif on back, then rep from * to * down to motif at lower edge of back, 1dc into each dc (2dc, 2ch and 2dc) into corner sp, 1dc into each dc across first motif, 1dc into each of next 2sp, 1dc into each dc across second motif on lower edge of back, (2dc, 2ch and 2dc) into corner sp, now work up other side of back, across shoulders and down side edge to match. Turn.
2nd row 3ch, skip first dc, 1dc into each dc to end, working (2dc, 2ch and 2dc) into each of corners on lower edge of back. Rep last row, working 1 row white, 1 row pink and 1 row white. Fasten off.

Left sleeve
With RS facing join green to 20th dc from shoulder seam on left front, 3ch, 1dc into each of next 19dc, then work 1dc into each of next 20dc on back. Turn. 40dc. Now work 1 row white, 1 row yellow, 1 row white, 1 row pink, 1 row green

bobbles, 1 row pink, 2 rows white, 1 row yellow bobbles, 1 row white, 2 rows blue and 1 row picot in blue.

Right sleeve
Work as for left sleeve but join yarn to 20th dc on back.

To finish
With WS tog, match row ends, leaving two motifs at lower edge of back free for flap. Join blue to lower edge of left side and working through the double thickness work 1sc into each of first 3dc, *3ch, sl st into last sc worked, 1sc into each of next 3sts, rep from * along left side edge to sleeve, join sleeve seam by working (2sc into next row end, 1sc into next row end, 3ch, sl st into last sc worked) to end of sleeve. Fasten off. Join other sleeve seam and side seam in the same way but start at sleeve seam.

Front and neck edging
With RS facing join blue to first row end on right front and work *2sc into next row end, 1sc into next row end, 3ch, sl st into last sc worked, rep from * up to motif, **1sc into each of next 3dc, 3ch, sl st into last sc worked, rep from ** to shoulder, then rep from * across shoulder row ends, then from ** across back neck sts, from * across shoulder row ends and from ** down other motif, then from * down remainder of left front edge. Fasten off.
Sew in zipper. Turn up lower flap, mark button positions, then sew on buttons using spaces in crochet for buttonholes. Work picot edging around flap in blue following the directions in Technique tip.

Technique tip

Picot edging

Picots form a simple but decorative edging for garments and household items. A picot edging can be worked on both knitted and crocheted fabrics.

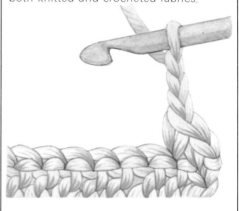

Join on yarn and work 2 single crochets, now work 3 chains for the picot; the number of chains can vary according to the size of the picot desired.

To form the picot, work a slip stitch into the top of the last single crochet worked. This completes the picot.

Work 3 single crochets and a picot along edge of work.

Black is beautiful

Especially when you use a soft mohair yarn and decorate it with beads and sequins.

Sizes
To fit 32[34:36]in (83[87:92]cm) bust.
Length, 22[22½:23]in (56[57:58]cm).
Sleeve seam, 17[17½:18]in (43[45:46]cm).

Note: Directions for larger sizes are in brackets []; if there is only one set of figures it applies to all sizes.

Materials
10[10:11]oz (270[270:300]g) of a lightweight mohair yarn
1 pair No. 2 (3mm) knitting needles
4in (10cm) lightweight zipper
Sequins and beads for decoration

Gauge
28 sts and 36 rows to 4in (10cm) in stockinette st.

Back
*Using No. 2 (3mm) needles cast on 104[112:120] sts. Work 4 rows K1, P1 ribbing. Beg with a K row, cont in stockinette st, dec one st at each end of 3rd and every foll 4th row until 94[102:108] sts rem. Cont straight until work measures 3¼in (8cm); end with a P row. Now inc one st at each end of 7th and every foll 6th row until there are 120[126:134] sts. Cont straight until work measures 15in (38cm); end with a P row.

Shape armholes
Bind off 8 sts at beg of next 2 rows. Dec one st at each end of every foll alternate row until 88[90:94] sts rem. Cont straight until armhole measures 4¼[4¾:5]in (11[12:13]cm); end with a P row.*

Divide for back opening
Next row K43[44:46], turn and leave rem sts on a spare needle.
Cont on first set of sts until armhole measures 7[7½:8]in (18[19:20]cm); end at armhole edge.

Shape shoulder
Bind off 7 sts at beg of next and foll 2 alternate rows and 5[5:7] sts at beg of foll alternate row. Work 1 row. Bind off.
Rejoin yarn to inner end of sts on spare needle, bind off 2 sts and K to end of row. Complete to match first side.

Front
Work as for back from * to *.

Divide for neck
Next row K44[45:47], turn and leave rem sts on a spare needle.
Next row K1, P to end.
Next row K.
Next row K1, P to end.
Rep last 2 rows 6 times more.
Next row K to last 5 sts, (K2 tog) twice, K1.
Next row K1, P to end.

☐ = 1 bead
○ = 1 sequin

Next row K.
Next row K1, P to end.
Rep last 4 rows once more.
Next row K to last 5 sts, (K2 tog) twice, K1.
Next row K1, P to end.
Next row Bind off 7, K to end.
Next row K1, P to end.
Next row Bind off 7, K to last 5 sts, (K2 tog) twice, K1.
Next row K1, P to end.
Next row Bind off 7, K to end.
Next row K1, P to end.
Next row Bind off 5[5:7], K to end. 10[11:11] sts.
Next row K1, P to end.
Next row K.
Rep last 2 rows until band fits from shoulder, along back neck edge to back neck opening, ending with a WS row. Bind off. Rejoin yarn to inner end of sts on spare needle.
Next row K.
Next row P to last st, K1.
Rep last 2 rows 7 times more.
Next row K1, (sl 1, K1, psso) twice, K to end.
Next row P to last st, K1.
Next row K.
Next row P to last st, K1.
Rep last 4 rows once more.
Next row K1, (sl 1, K1, psso) twice, K to end.
Next row P to last st, K1.
Next row K.
Next row Bind off 7, P to last st, K1.
Next row K1, (sl 1, K1, psso) twice, K to end.
Next row Bind off 7, P to last st, K1.

Next row K.
Rep last 2 rows once.
Next row Bind off 5[5:7], P to last st, K1. 10[11:11] sts.
Next row K.
Next row P to last st, K1.
Rep last 2 rows until band fits from shoulder, along back neck edge to back neck opening, ending with a WS row. Bind off.

Sleeves
Using No. 2 (3mm) needles cast on 50[52:54] sts. Work 4 rows K1, P1 ribbing.
Beg with a K row, cont in stockinette st, inc one st at each end of 9th and every foll 8th[8th:7th] row until there are 84[88:92] sts. Cont straight until work measures 17[17½:18]in (43[45:46]cm); end with a P row.

Shape top
Bind off 8 sts at beg of next 2 rows. Dec one st at each end of every row until 54[58:62] sts rem. Work 26[28:32] rows straight. Now dec one st at each end of next and every foll alternate row until 40[44:48] sts rem, then each end of every row until 28 sts rem. Bind off.

To finish
Join shoulder seams. Sew back neckband to neck edge. With RS facing, using No. 2 (3mm) needles pick up and K 62 sts evenly along back neck opening. Bind off. Set in sleeves, gathering sleeve cap to form "puff." Join side and sleeve seams. Sew in zipper. Follow chart for design and sew sequins and beads to front.

EXTRA SPECIAL KNITTING

When it's time for bed, small feet won't feel the cold inside these slipper socks. When they're finished, add an embroidered motif and sew or glue on leather soles to prevent wear.

Cozy toes

Sizes
Leg, 9[11]in (23[28]cm).
Foot, 7½[9]in (19[23]cm).
Note Directions for larger size are in brackets [ ]; if there is only one set of figures it applies to both sizes.

Materials
3oz (75g) of a knitting worsted (A)
4oz (100g) of a knitting worsted (B)
Scraps of knitting worsted for embroidery in two colors (C and D)
1 pair each Nos. 6 and 8 (4½ and 5½mm) knitting needles
Leather for soles

Gauge
15 sts and 19 rows to 4in (10cm) in stockinette st on No. 8 (5½mm) needles

To make
Using No. 6 (4½mm) needles and A, cast on 62[74] sts.
1st row K2, *P2, K2, rep from * to end.
2nd row P2, *K2, P2, rep from * to end.
Rep these 2 rows for 9[11]in (23[28]cm); with a 2nd row. Cut off A.
With RS facing sl first 18[22] sts onto a holder, change to No. 8 (5½mm) needles, join on B and (K2 tog), 13[15] times, turn and leave rem sts on a spare needle.
Cont on these 13[15] sts in stockinette st for 4¼[5½]in (11[14]cm); end with a P row.
Next row K1, sl 1, K1, psso, K to last 3 sts, K2 tog, K1.
Next row P to end.
Rep these 2 rows twice more. 7[9] sts. Cut off yarn. Sl the first 18[22] sts from holder back onto left-hand needle. Using No. 8 (5½mm) needles and B, (K2 tog) 9[11] times, pick up and K 17[21] sts along side of foot, K the 7[9] toe sts, pick up and K 17[21] sts along other side of foot, then (K2 tog) 9[11] times across rem sts. K 5 rows. Cut off yarn. With RS facing sl the first 27[33] sts onto right-hand needle, join in the second ball of B and work the sole with 2 strands of B tog, K5[7], turn, K6[8], turn, K7[9] turn. Cont to work one more st on every row until the row K11[13], turn has been worked.
Next row Sl 1, K9[11], K2 tog tbl, turn.
Rep last row until 6[7] sts rem unworked at each end of row.
Next row K10[12], turn, K9[11], turn.
Cont to work one st less on every row until the row K5[7], turn has been worked.
Sl all sts back onto left-hand needle and bind off across all sts.
Make other sock in the same way.

To finish
Do not press. Join seam at heel, then join seam at back of leg, reversing seam at top for turn-over. Work duplicate stitch on foot as in photo. Cut leather to shape, then glue or sew to sole of sock.

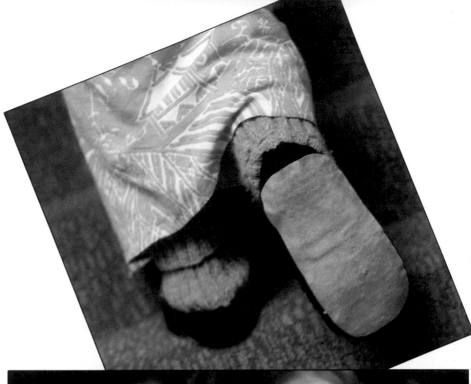

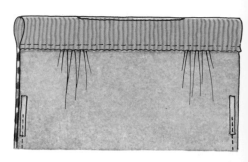

Talk of the town

A clever combination of knitting and sewing, this dress is shaped by the bands of knitted fabric sewn into it at the waist, yoke and cuffs. The outfit is completed with a hat with a band of knitting around it.

Measurements Sizes 10/12 and 14/16. Measurements for the larger size are given in brackets []. If only one measurement is given, it applies to both sizes.

Suggested fabrics
The dress should be made in a fabric which has some body but is also soft and fluid, such as single knits, crepe or lightweight wool.

Materials
$4\frac{1}{8}$yd (3.8m) of 36in (90cm)-wide
  fabric or
$3\frac{1}{4}$yd (2.9m) of 45in (115cm)-wide
  fabric or
$2\frac{1}{2}[2\frac{5}{8}]$yd (2.2m [2.3m]) of 54/60in
  (140/150cm)-wide fabric
Matching thread
$2\frac{1}{4}$yd (2m) seam tape
Yardstick, right triangle, flexible
  curve, dressmaker's chalk
For the knitted sections:
6oz (160g) of a sport yarn
1 pair No. 2 ($2\frac{3}{4}$mm) knitting needles

Knitted sections

Gauge
40 sts and 42 rows to 4in (10cm) in ribbing, worked on No. 2 ($2\frac{3}{4}$mm) needles.

Yoke
Cast on 189 [205] sts.
1st ribbing row (RS) K2, *P1, K1, rep from * to last st, K1.
2nd ribbing row K1, *P1, K1, rep from * to end.
Rep these 2 rows until work measures 3in (7.5cm). Bind off in ribbing.
Make another piece in the same way.

Waistbands
Cast on 133[141] sts.
Rep the 2 ribbing rows as given for yoke until work measures $3\frac{1}{4}$ (8.5cm). Bind off in ribbing.
Make another piece in the same way.

Cuffs
Cast on 81 sts. Rep the 2 ribbing rows as given for yoke until work measures 3in (7.5cm). Bind off. Make another piece in the same way.

Cutting out

1 Using a yardstick, a right triangle, a flexible curve and dressmaker's chalk, mark the pattern pieces on the fabric, following the appropriate measurement diagram and cutting layout. The bodice and pockets will be easier to cut if you make a paper pattern first.

Making the garment

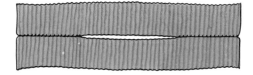

1 Start by joining the two knitted yoke sections (sewn by hand): with right sides facing, use a flat seam to join the two bound-off edges together for 5[$5\frac{1}{2}$]in (13[14]cm) to form shoulder seams.

2 The front and back bodice sections are gathered slightly to give the dress fullness. On the front bodice section, run two lines of gathering stitches, positioning each pair 3[$3\frac{1}{4}$]in (8[8.5]cm) from center front and making each section 4in (10cm) long.
3 On the back bodice, position gathers $4\frac{3}{4}$[5]in (12[12.5]cm) from center back, again making them 4in (10cm) long. Draw up both sets of gathers so that the width of the upper edge of the bodice front and back matches the width of the knitted sections. Stitch the seam as described in Technique Tip, page 105.

4 To strengthen the seam at the underarm point, cut four 2in (5cm) lengths of seam tape and pin to side seams of bodice at underarm points. With right sides together and raw edges matching, pin, baste and stitch side seams as far as underarm point, catching 1in (2.5cm) of seam tape at the top of the seam.

5 Pin, baste and stitch sleeve seams, right sides together and raw edges matching, leaving $\frac{5}{8}$in (1.5cm) unstitched at armhole edge. Pin sleeve into armhole, matching sleeve seam with side seam. Stitch from underarm point and around sleeve cap (without stretching the knitting) and back to underarm point, without stitching across the seamline. Catch in the seam tape as you stitch.
6 Clip into the side seam allowance at underarm point, without clipping the tape. Finish the raw edges.
7 Join cuff pieces to form rings and the two waist pieces at the short ends.
8 Attach cuffs to lower ends of sleeves (see Technique Tip).
9 Stitch center back seam of skirt.

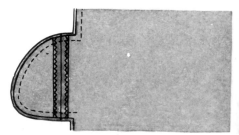

10 With right sides together and raw edges matching, join each pocket piece to one of the pocket extensions, using a flat seam. Press seam open. Finish seam allowances. Pin and baste front skirt section to back section, matching pocket shapes. Stitch side seams for 7in (18cm) from upper raw edge. Keeping the needle in the fabric, turn and stitch around pocket. Stitch $\frac{5}{8}$in (1.5cm) into the seam

allowance of the skirt at the lower edge of the pocket as shown.

11 Leaving a pocket opening of 6¼in (16cm), stitch rest of side seam, starting 13⅜in (34cm) from top of skirt, stitching down to the hem edge. Finish seam edges, finishing seams around pockets together. Press pocket forward. Press remainder of seam open.

12 Join bodice and skirt sections to waistband, following Technique Tip, stretching the knitted strip as you stitch. Do not press the knitted section or the ribbing will lose its elasticity.

13 Try dress on and turn up hem; sew hem by hand.

Note On page 107, you will find directions for making the hat that goes with this dress, along with a range of variations to top the outfit.

Jean-Claude Volpeliere

Diagram labels:
- 6¼[7] in
- 5[5¼] in
- 19¼[20⅞] in
- 1⅜in
- ⅜in
- 6¾[7] in underarm point
- 15¾[16½] in
- BODICE BACK AND FRONT cut 2 on fold
- SLEEVE cut 2
- 10⅝[11⅜] in
- 5¾in
- 8¼[9¼] in
- 6¼in
- 11in
- SKIRT FRONT cut 1 on fold
- 34½[35¼] in
- 1¼in

Technique tip

Sewing hand-knitted fabric by machine.

The knitted panels in this dress are joined to the rest of the garment with a machine-stitched seam.

There are a few simple techniques which are useful when stitching knitted fabric, depending on the position of the seam and the stress it has to take.

Evenly gathered seam

Often hand-knitted sections are used because they are more elastic than ordinary fabrics, so that there is no need for openings and fastenings. The simplest type of gathered seam is made when the knitted strip, fully stretched, matches the length of the raw edge of the garment fabric, as at the waist of this dress.

At the cuffs, the garment fabric is too full to match to the stretched cuff section. Run a couple of lines of gathering stitches through the lower edge of the sleeve and draw it up slightly before stitching the seam.

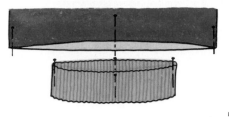

Divide the garment fabric into four and mark with pins. Repeat on the knitted section.

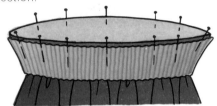

Pin together the two sections to be joined, with right sides facing and marked points matching. Stitch with the knitted section up, stretching it as you stitch, using a zigzag or stretch stitch.

Regulated gathers

On the yoke of the dress, the amount of "give" in the hand-knitted section has to be restricted to prevent the yoke from sagging, but at the same time there must be some gathers in the garment fabric to give fullness where it is needed. In this case, the seam is strengthened with tape.

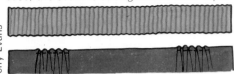

Gather the woven fabric, distributing fullness according to the pattern directions. The knitted section, unstretched, should be the same length as the gathered garment fabric for a neat fit. Cut a piece of seam tape to fit the width of the knitted section.

Pin and baste the knitted section to the gathered garment fabric, attaching the tape at the same time on the wrong side of the knitted section. Machine stitch through all three layers without stretching the knitted section.

Measurement diagram

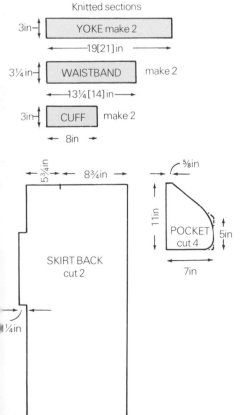

Knitted sections

- 3in — YOKE make 2 — 19[21] in
- 3¼ in — WAISTBAND — make 2 — 13¼ [14] in
- 3in — CUFF — make 2 — 8in

5¾in · 8¾in · ⅝in

11in · POCKET cut 4 · 5in · 7in

SKIRT BACK cut 2 · 1¼ in

Cutting layout for 45in-wide fabric

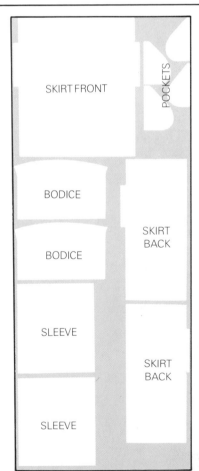

SKIRT FRONT · POCKETS · BODICE · BODICE · SKIRT BACK · SLEEVE · SKIRT BACK · SLEEVE

54/60in-wide fabric

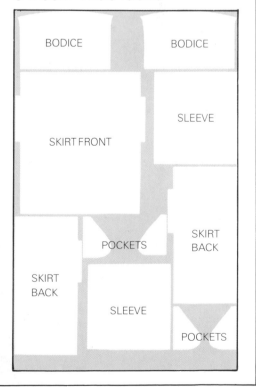

BODICE · BODICE · SLEEVE · SKIRT FRONT · POCKETS · SKIRT BACK · SKIRT BACK · SLEEVE · POCKETS

If you want to get ahead

. . . these hats are just the ticket! Fashioned from a small piece of wool fabric with a knitted band around the edge, they are surprisingly easy to make — a simple introduction to the milliner's craft.

Finished size
The finished size of the hat depends on the size of the form you buy: choose a shallow form to fit the crown of your head.

Materials
    A simple, domed hat form (these are available from notions departments)
    ½yd (.5m) of loosely woven wool fabric
    Scrap of contrasting fabric (optional)
    ⅜yd (.3m) of thick filler cord (optional)
    ½yd (.5m) of lining fabric (optional)
    Fabric glue, matching thread
    For the knitted band: 5oz (125g) of a sport yarn
    1 pair of No. 2 (2¾mm) knitting needles

Gauge
40 sts to 4in (10cm), measured over K1, P1 ribbing on No. 2 (2¾mm) needles.
Note: Precise measurements cannot be given; when making hats it is necessary to work to the form you are using: the fabric is eased over the form and then trimmed as necessary. Professionals use a block to put the hat form on while stretching the fabric, but this is not necessary for a simple hat like the one shown here. However, you may find it useful to put the hat form on a wig stand while you are working on it.

Plain version

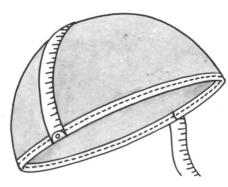

1 Measure over the crown of the hat form to estimate the diameter of the fabric circle to be cut. Cut a circle of fabric 3in (7.5cm) larger in diameter than the crown measurement.
2 Mark the center front and center back of the hat form. (Most forms are not quite circular.) Mark the diagonal (bias) grain of the fabric with a line of basting stitches.

Terry Evans

3 Place the fabric over the crown, matching the basted line to the marks at the front and back. Pin in place.

Victor Yuan

4 Ease the fullness out of the circle of fabric, pinning it to the hat form at regular intervals. Baste in position close to edge of hat form and remove pins.

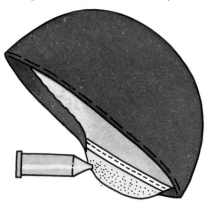

5 Trim fabric so that $\frac{5}{8}$in (1.5cm) extends beyond edge of hat form. Turn fabric under and glue in place.

6 To calculate the width of the ribbing, measure around edge of the hat form. Multiply the measurement by 4: this gives the number of stitches to cast on.

1st row K1, *K1, P1, rep from * to last st, K1.

2nd row K1, *K1, P1, rep from * to last st, K1.

Continue in ribbing until work measures $4\frac{3}{4}$in (12cm). Bind off.

7 Join short ends of ribbed knitting. Butt ribbing to edge of hat, positioning seam at center back, and slip stitch cast-on edge to lower edge of hat. The ribbing extends below the covered hat form and turns up or rolls up to form a brim.

8 If you wish, line the hat. Cut a circle of lining fabric 2in (5cm) in diameter. Glue it inside crown of hat. Cut a bias strip of fabric about 4in (10cm) wide and as long as the circumference of the hat, plus $1\frac{1}{4}$in (3cm) seam allowance. Join the two ends with a flat seam.

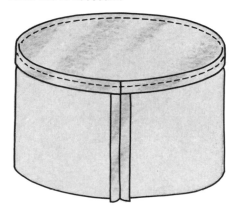

9 Turn under and stitch $\frac{3}{8}$in (1cm) along one long edge. Run a line of gathering stitches through finished edge. Pull up to form ring about $1\frac{1}{2}$in (4cm) in diameter.

10 Place lining inside hat and pin it in place. Catch-stitch gathered edge to circle glued into crown. Trim away excess fabric, leaving $\frac{3}{8}$in (1cm) extending beyond edge of hat. Turn under $\frac{5}{8}$in (1.5cm); slip stitch to edge of cover fabric.

Corded version

To add interest to the hat, a strip of cording can be sewn over the crown.

1 Cut a circle of fabric to cover the hat, making its diameter 4in (10cm) larger than the crown measurement. Fold the circle in half on the bias and cut.

2 Cut a strip of contrasting fabric on the bias, making it $2\frac{3}{8}$in (6cm) longer than the crown measurement. Cut a length of cord $\frac{3}{8}$in (1cm) shorter than crown measurement.

3 Baste and stitch the crown seam, enclosing the cording. Enclose the ends of the bias strip in the seam so that they are finished as you stitch the seam.

4 Mark the front and back of the hat form.

5 Complete the hat as from step 3 of the plain version, matching the seamline to the marks at the front and back of the hat form.

Variations

Once you have made the basic hat, with or without cording, you might try a few simple variations that will change the look of the hat.

1 Cut a strip of fiberfill $1\frac{1}{4}$in (3cm) deep by the circumference of the hat. Catch-stitch to knitted band so that when you turn up the brim it is given extra bulk.

2 Select a few beautiful feathers and bind the ends with a scrap of fabric. Either sew the feathers in place or pin them with a brooch.

3 Run a line of gathering stitches through one long edge of a piece of net about 6–12in (15–30cm) deep and 36in (90cm)-wide. Catch-stitch to the edge of the hat.

4 Remove the knitted band altogether.

Needlework EXTRA

A traditional symbol of hospitality, the pineapple is a beautiful fruit that makes a good subject for embroidery. Our pineapple picture is worked in tent stitch on fine canvas.

Welcome motif

Finished size: 6×8in (15×20cm).

Materials
*Piece of No. 22 canvas, preferably
pale yellow, 10×12in (25×30cm)
D.M.C. stranded embroidery floss, 1
skein each of the following colors:
319, 367, 368, 996, 369 (greens);
300, 400, 780, 420, 782 (browns);
783, 972, 725 (golds); 322, 312
(blues); 355, 919, 356, 920, 301,
922, 921, 976, 977, 946, 971, 970
(rusts and oranges—use any or all
of these); 108 (shaded orange-
gold)*

*No. 24 tapestry needle; button thread
Piece of cardboard 6×8in (15×20cm)*

Note: You can make the picture larger or
smaller by using a different gauge of
canvas and adjusting the needle and
thread thickness.

Making the picture
1 Bind the edges of the canvas with
masking tape. Mark the upper edge of the
finished picture with a 6in (15cm) line
about 2in (5cm) from the bound edge.
2 Using three strands of thread in the
needle, work the embroidery following

the chart below. Begin with the
uppermost leaf, worked in shade 369,
placing the point of the leaf 16 threads
down from the marked upper edge. Work
all the leaves first, following color key.
3 Now work the main part of the
pineapple. The designer has used many
different shades for a subtle effect; the
simplified chart shows the outlines of the
segments and the main colors within
them. You can use as much or as little
detail as you like. First work the darker
outlines, as shown on the chart, using the
colors indicated by the key. Then fill in
the shapes, using the colors of your

choice. Use continental tent stitch (see Volume 1, page 69) for the pineapple.
4 Now, using the basketweave form of tent stitch (see Volume 1, page 69), work the table top in the two shades of blue, up to the level shown in the photograph, finishing 8in (20cm) below the marked upper edge.

Leave the background unworked, if you like, or fill it in with tent stitch in a color, or colors, of your choice.
5 When the embroidery is completed, remove the tape and block it (see Volume 1, page 72).
6 To mount the embroidery on the cardboard, place it face down on a clean

surface, place the cardboard on top and, using button thread, lace the two long edges together, sewing through first one edge and then the other. Repeat with the two short edges, making sure the corners are turned neatly.
7 Frame the embroidery as desired.

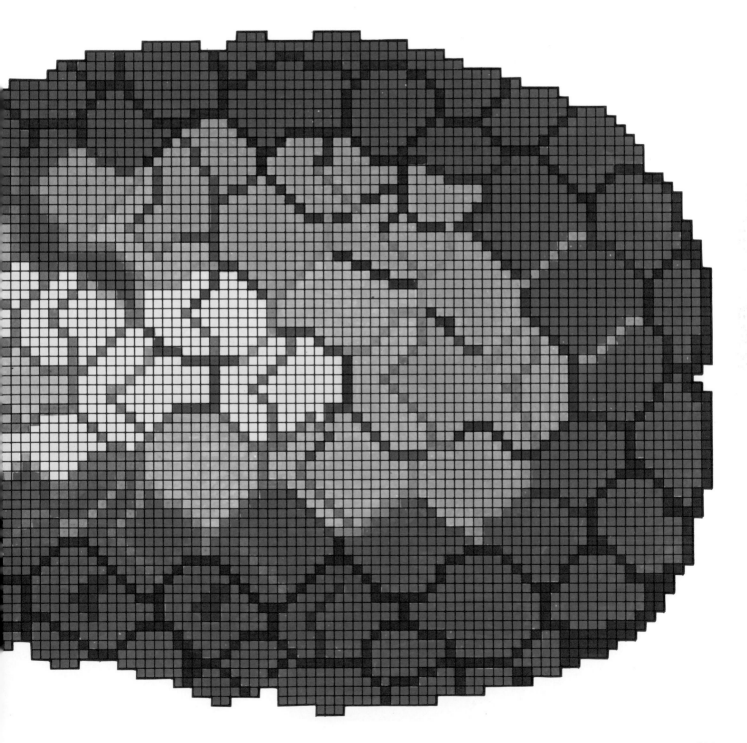

Homemaker

Hide-away mattress

This foam-filled mattress will be comfortable enough for a young overnight guest and when it is not in use, it will fold up neatly into its own cover. And, as an extra-large floor pillow, it's a useful addition to a teenager's bedroom. To keep it off the floor and out of the way, we've added plastic rings.

Finished sizes
Mattress is about 67 × 35in (170 × 90cm).
Cover is 37½in (96cm) square.
A seam allowance of ¾in (2cm) has been included throughout.

Materials
5½yd (5m) of 48in (122cm)-wide sturdy cotton fabric
1⅛yd (1m) of 45in (115cm)-wide cotton poplin in two colors
2¼yd (2m) of 45in (115cm)-wide lightweight polyester batting
2¼yd (2m) of 45in (115cm)-wide lightweight fabric for lining
4¾yd (4m) of extra thick filler cord
Two 3¼in (8.5cm)-diameter plastic rings; foam chips for stuffing
Seven ⅝in (1.5cm)-diameter snaps
Matching thread

Mattress

1 From sturdy cotton fabric cut out two pieces, 85½ × 37in (215 × 94cm) for mattress pieces.

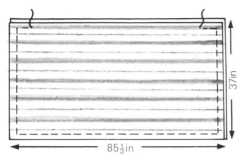

2 Place mattress pieces together with right sides facing and edges matching.

Starting 1in (2.5cm) from corner on one long side, pin, baste and stitch toward short edge, then turn and continue around mattress until you reach the first long side again, and stitch for another 1in (2.5cm).

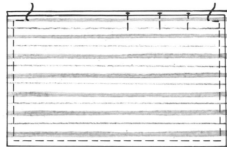

3 Measure 6in (15cm) along open long side, starting from seam at short end, and

mark. Continue marking points at 6in (15cm) intervals along this edge.

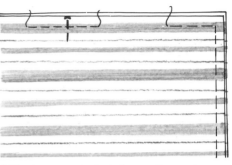

Birgit Webb

4 Pin, baste and stitch the mattress pieces together on the open side for 1in (2.5cm) on each side of each marked point, excluding the last two marks, so leaving a large enough gap for turning.

Kim Sayer

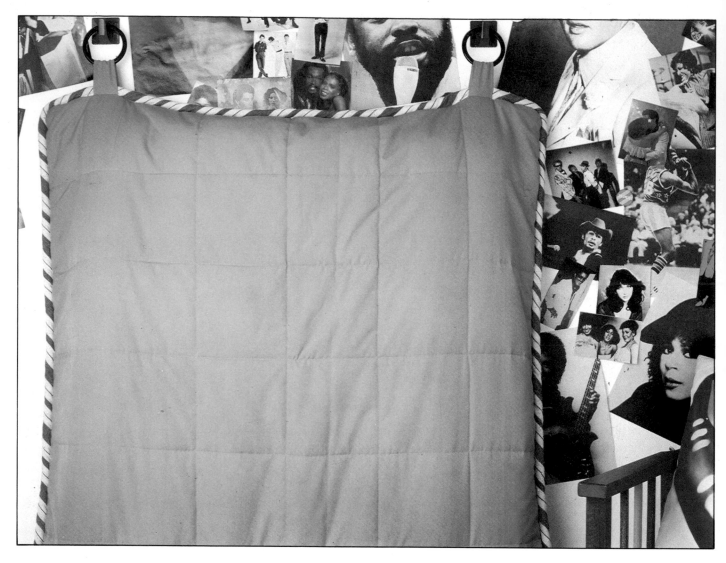

5 Trim seams, cut diagonally across corners and turn mattress right side out.

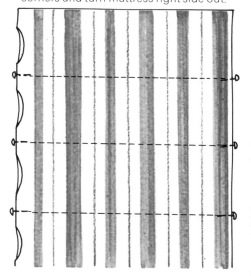

6 Starting at one short end of the mattress, mark points 6in (15cm) apart on each long side along the entire length. Pin, baste and stitch across the mattress at each set of marked points, forming channels for the stuffing.

7 At the two open channels, turn under the seam allowance on the open edge before stitching across the mattress.
8 Fill each channel with foam chips. Turn in edges and pin.

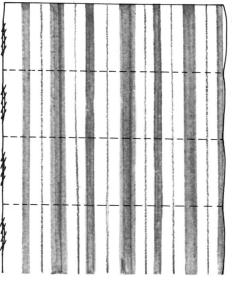

9 Slip stitch folded edges of each channel opening together.

Mattress cover

1 Trim each piece of plain poplin to make 39in (100cm) squares.
2 From batting and lining fabric cut out two 39in (100cm) squares. (If only narrower widths of batting are available, buy extra and piece to make up squares.)

3 Fold one poplin piece in half both ways into quarters and mark center point. Mark the two fold lines across the poplin.

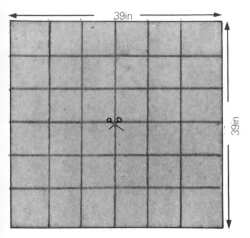

4 Working outward from each center line, measure and mark eight more lines, 6¼in (16cm) apart. The outer lines will be 7in (18cm) from the edges.

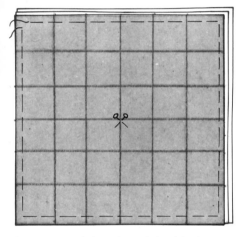

5 Place one lining piece right side down and lay a square of batting on it. Lay a square of poplin on top, right side up. Pin and baste fabrics together around all four edges.

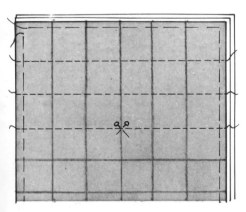

6 Stitch the three fabrics together along the marked lines.
7 Repeat steps 3 to 6 to make the other side of cover, using contrasting poplin.
8 For cording, from the mattress fabric cut out 3in (8cm) -wide strips on the bias of the fabric. Pin, baste and stitch the strips together along the straight grain (diagonal edges) to make a strip 4⅜yd (4m) long.

9 Fold the bias strip in half around the cord, wrong side inside and edges matching. Pin, baste and stitch; using cording foot, close to the cord, leaving 4in (10cm) free at each end.
10 Cut four pieces of poplin—either color—for hangers, each 5×7in (13×18cm). Place them in pairs to make a double thickness.

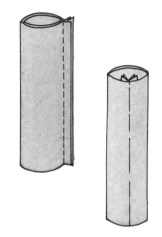

11 Fold one double hanger piece in half lengthwise; pin, baste and stitch long edges together. Trim and turn hanger right side out. Press seam over center.
12 Repeat step 11 to make other hanger in the same way.

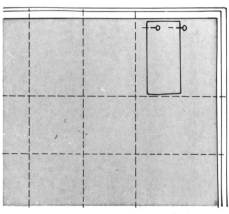

13 Pin one short edge of each hanger piece to matching cover piece, 5in (13cm) in from side edges.

14 Pin the cording around the edges of the same cover piece, starting at the center of the edge opposite hangers. Trim cord ends and sew together. Overlap fabric ends, turning in raw edge on top piece; slip stitch in place.
15 Slip the hangers through the plastic rings. Pin free end of each hanger to cover piece over cording.
16 Baste and stitch the cording and hangers in place around all four edges of the cover piece.
17 From the other piece of poplin cut two pieces, each 37½×2¼in (96×6cm), for binding the opening edges.

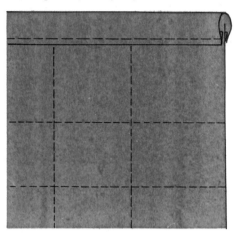

18 Turn in ⅜in (1cm) on long edges of one binding piece. Fold strip in half, wrong sides inside, over hanger edge of corded cover piece. Pin, baste and stitch the strip in place.
19 Repeat step 18 to bind one edge of the other piece in the same way.

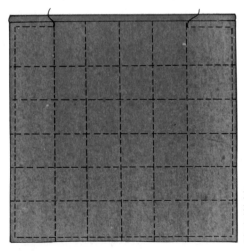

20 Place the cover pieces together, right sides facing and bound edges matching. Pin, baste and stitch around cover just outside cording, starting at bound edge, on first line of quilting, and ending at first line on opposite side. Trim seams; cut diagonally across corners. Turn cover right side out.
21 Sew snap fasteners along the bound edges, positioning them at intervals of about 3in (7.5cm).

Birgit Webb

Homemaker

Box of tricks

Line an old box with a pretty quilted fabric and in next to no time you have a blanket box. Then top it with a cushion.

Finished size

This box is 29½in (75cm) long, 16in (40cm) wide and 14½in (37cm) tall; directions can be adapted for other chests. A ¾in (2cm) seam allowance is included.

Materials

2½yd (2.3m) of 48in (122cm)-wide quilted print fabric
1⅛yd (1m) of 48in (122cm)-wide matching unquilted fabric
1⅛yd (1m) of 36in (90cm)-wide solid-color fabric
11yd (10m) of filler cord
5½yd (5m) of ⅝in (1.5cm)-wide Velcro®
Piece of 2in (5cm)-thick foam, 31½×17in (80×43cm)
Fabric glue; matching thread

Measuring and cutting out

1 The box lining is made from three pieces—one main piece and two end panels.

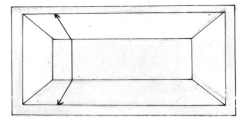

2 For the main piece, measure inside the box, from the top down the back, across the base and up the front to the top front edge. Measure the inside length, from one end to the other. Add 1½in (4cm) to both measurements for seam allowance. Cut out one quilted piece this size.

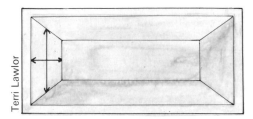

3 For the end panels, measure the inside width of the box. Measure the height of the box. Add 1½in (4cm) to both measurements for seam allowance. Cut out two pieces of quilted fabric this size.

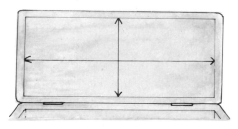

4 For the lid lining, measure the length and width of the inside of the lid. Add 2½in (6cm) to both measurements for 1¼in (3cm) hems. Cut out one piece of quilted fabric this size.

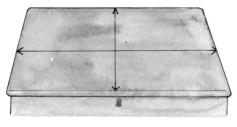

5 For the cushion, measure the length and width of the outside of the lid. Cut out one piece of foam to fit these measurements.

6 For cushion cover, add 1½in (4cm) to both cushion measurements for seam allowance. Cut out two pieces of unquilted fabric this size. For the gusset, measure all around the edge of the foam, measure the depth and add 1½in (4cm) to both measurements for seam allowance. Cut out one piece of unquilted fabric this size.

To make the box and lid linings

1 For the cording, cut out 2in (5cm)-wide strips of solid-color fabric, cutting them on the bias.

2 Pin, baste and stitch them together to form an 11yd (10m)-long strip.

3 Fold bias strip around cord with wrong side inside and edges matching. Pin and baste along the length of the cording, close to the cord.
4 Cut two lengths of cording to fit each long edge of main lining piece.

5 Place one length of cording on the right side of the main piece, with the cord toward the center and the line of basting on the seam line $\frac{3}{4}$in (2cm) from the edge. Pin and baste in place.
6 Repeat step 5 on the opposite long side of the main piece.

7 Mark the center point on each long side of the main piece.
8 Mark the center point on upper and lower edges of each end panel.

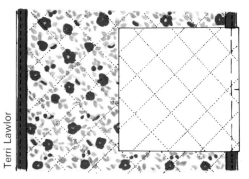

Terri Lawlor

9 Matching center points, place one end panel on one long side of main piece, with right sides together and raw edges matching, enclosing the cording. Pin and baste in place.
10 Repeat step 9 on the opposite long side of the main piece.

11 At one corner of lining, match up the corner point of end panel and the corner point of the main piece with right sides together and edges matching. Pin and baste this seam from the corner to the seam along the bottom.
12 Repeat step 11 to match up all the corner points in turn and form the box shape for the lining. Pin and baste each of the seams.
13 Put the lining inside the box and check for fit. Alter the seams if necessary. Stitch all the seams together along basted lines.
14 To finish the seams, trim away the batting in the quilted fabric from the seam, leaving only the fabric. Turn under the raw edge of the fabric and hand-hem it in place, covering the edge of the batting neatly.
15 Trim the cording seam allowance to $\frac{3}{8}$in (2cm) and overcast the edges together to finish them.

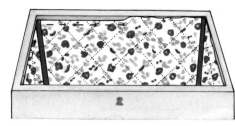

16 Place the lining inside the box. Turn the top edge to the wrong side and pin in place, so that there is a gap of $\frac{3}{8}$in (1cm) between the folded edge and the top of the box. Remove the lining from the box. Mark the foldline all around the top edge of the lining with a line of small basting stitches.
17 Cut a length of cording to fit around the top edge of the lining, allowing for joining.
18 Position the cording on the right side of the top edge of the lining with the cord toward the center, just inside the line of basting. Join cording ends to fit. Pin, baste and stitch the cording in place. Trim away the batting from the seam allowance all around the top edge to reduce unnecessary bulk.
19 Cut four pieces of Velcro®: two pieces the length of the long sides, less $\frac{3}{4}$in (2cm) and two pieces the length of the short sides less $\frac{3}{4}$in (2cm).

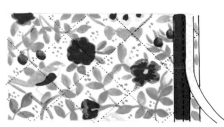

20 Place the furry half of one long piece of Velcro® on the seam allowance.

on one long edge of the lining, placing it alongside the cording (over the raw edge of the cording fabric) with the edge about $\frac{1}{8}$in (3mm) from the basted fitting line and $\frac{3}{8}$in (1cm) in from each corner seam. Pin, baste and stitch the edge nearest the cording in place.
21 Repeat step 20 to apply the remaining lengths of Velcro®.
22 Trim the seam allowance on each side, so that the raw edge is hidden under the fastening strips.
23 Fold the fabric to the wrong side along the marked line on the top edge. Pin, baste and hem the Velcro® to the quilted fabric by hand.
24 Place the lining in the box and mark the positions of Velcro® strips.

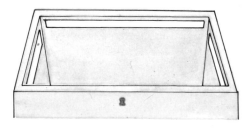

25 Glue the opposite half of each length of Velcro® to the box, so that they correspond to the strips on the fabric.

26 On the lid lining, pin the $1\frac{1}{4}$in (3cm) to the wrong side, making neat corners. Place the lining inside the lid and check for fit; adjust if necessary. Remove the lining from the lid. Mark the foldlines with small basting stitches.
27 Cut four pieces of Velcro®: two pieces the length of the long side and two pieces the length of the short side.

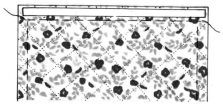

28 Place the furry half of one long strip of Velcro® on the seam allowance of one long side, placing it about $\frac{1}{8}$in (3mm) from the line of basting. Baste in place.
29 Repeat step 28 to baste each length of Velcro® in place close to the foldline, trimming them if necessary to fit at the corners.
30 Trim away the batting on the seam allowance and trim the fabric also, so that so that the raw edges are hidden under the Velcro® strips.

31 Fold the fabric to the wrong side along the marked lines. Pin and hem the Velcro strips by hand to the quilted fabric.

32 Position the lining on the inside of the lid.

Mark the positions of the fastenings.

33 Glue the opposite half of each length of Velcro® to the lid, so that each strip corresponds to the strips on the fabric.

34 Fix both linings in place.

To make the cushion

1 Cut the remaining length of cording in half.

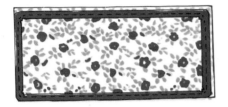

2 Position one length of cording around one cushion cover piece with the cording lying toward the center and the basting along the seamline.

Join cording together to fit. Pin and baste in place.

3 Repeat step 2 to baste cording around other cushion cover piece in the same way.

4 Pin, baste and stitch gusset strip to form a ring, placing right sides together and matching the raw edges.

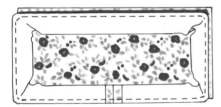

5 Place gusset on right side of one cushion cover piece over the cording, centering the gusset seam on one long side of the cover piece. Pin and baste in place.

6 Place other cover piece on opposite side of gusset in the same way. Pin and baste in place, leaving a 24in (60cm) opening in one long side.

7 Leaving the cushion cover wrong side out, place the foam inside the cover to check the fit. Adjust if necessary.

8 Remove the foam from the cover and stitch both seams. Trim seams and turn cover right side out. Insert the foam.

9 Turn in edges; slip stitch together.

Geoffrey Frosh

Homemaker

Kitchen chair cushions

Make kitchen chairs a bit more comfortable with these simple cushions. They're fastened on with toggles.

Size
As measured.

Materials (for 4 cushions)
Tracing paper and white paper
$3\frac{1}{8}$yd (2.8m) of 48in (122cm)-wide closely-woven furnishing fabric
Four pieces of $1\frac{1}{2}$in (4cm)-thick foam, 16in (40cm) square
8 toggles
1yd (1m) of $\frac{1}{4}$in (5mm)-wide elastic
Matching sewing thread
Sharp kitchen knife

1 Make a pattern of the chair seat. Lay a sheet of tracing paper over the seat and trace the front and side edges. At the back, continue the line in front of the struts and close to them, so that the cushion will fit snugly. Mark the positions of the struts to which the cushion will be fastened (see photo).
2 Remove the paper and cut out around the pattern. Fold the pattern in half lengthwise to check that it is symmetrical.

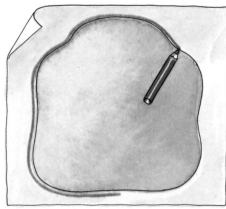

3 Place the pattern on a sheet of white paper and draw around it. Add $\frac{5}{8}$in (1.5cm)

seam allowance all around. Mark the fastening strut positions on the pattern. Mark the center back and center front of the cushion.
4 From fabric cut out eight cushion pieces. Mark the fastening struts and center back and front on each piece.
5 For length of gusset, measure around the pattern along the seamline and add $1\frac{1}{4}$in (3cm) to this measurement for the seam allowance.
6 Cut four strips to this measurement and $2\frac{3}{4}$in (7cm)-wide on the bias of fabric.
7 For fastening strips, cut out (piecing if necessary) a bias strip of fabric 63in (160cm) long and $1\frac{1}{2}$in (4cm) wide.

8 Fold the bias strip in half lengthwise. Pin, baste and stitch down the length, $\frac{3}{8}$in (1cm) from the edges. Trim and turn strip right side out.
9 For toggle fastening strips cut eight pieces, each 2in (5cm) long. For loop fastenings cut 8 pieces, each $5\frac{1}{2}$in (14cm) long. Cut eight pieces of elastic, each 4in (10cm) long, for loop fastenings. (Make eight sets in all.)

10 Thread a piece of elastic through one loop fastening strip, securing the elastic to fabric at both ends.

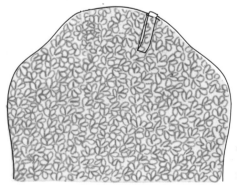

Terry Evans

11 Fold the loop in half, matching the ends. Pin and baste raw edges of loop to one inner strut position on back edge of one cushion piece, positioning it on the right side of the cushion piece, pointing inward.

12 Finish the raw edges on one end of a toggle fastening strip by turning them in for $\frac{3}{8}$in (1cm) and slip stitching them together.

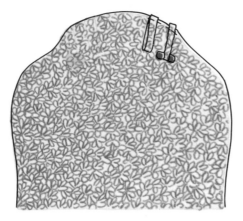

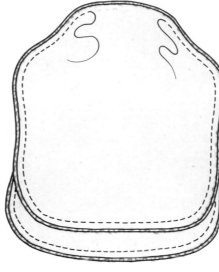

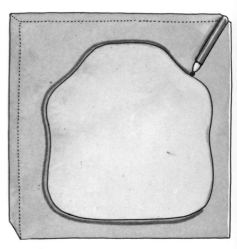

13 Pin and baste unfinished end of toggle fastening strip to one outer strut position on back edge of cushion piece, positioning it on right side, pointing inward. Sew fastening loop in place.
14 Repeat steps 10 to 13, pinning and basting second pair of fastenings to back of cushion piece in the remaining marked positions.

17 Pin remaining cushion piece to free long edge of gusset with right sides together and center backs aligned. Pin, baste and stitch, leaving a 7in (18cm) opening at the back of the cushion. Trim seam allowances and clip curves. Turn cushion right side out.
18 Sew a toggle to the end of each toggle fastening strip.

19 Trim seam allowance off the paper pattern. Place the trimmed pattern on one piece of foam and draw around it with a ballpoint pen. Using a kitchen knife or large scissors, cut the foam to the correct shape, following the marked line and taking care to make the cut vertical.
20 Insert the foam into the cushion cover. Turn in the opening edges and slip stitch them together.
21 Repeat steps 10 to 20 to make the remaining three cushions in the same way.

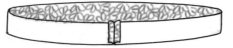

15 Pin, baste and stitch the short ends of one gusset piece to form a ring, placing right sides together and taking $\frac{5}{8}$in (1.5cm) seam allowance.

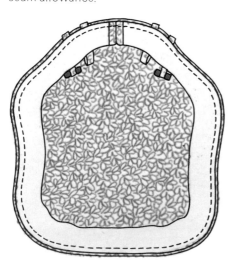

16 Place one long edge of gusset on cushion piece with fastenings, placing right sides together and aligning gusset seam and center back of cushion. Pin gusset in place, easing it to fit smoothly around the corners. Baste and stitch around the entire edge, catching in the fastening strips. Trim the seam allowances and clip into the curves so that the gusset will fit neatly around the curved edges of the cushion.

Homemaker
Topsy-turvy doll

At one end I'm sad, but turn me up and I'll be smiling!

Belinda/Designed by Jane Iles

Finished size
About 19in (48cm) tall.
A seam allowance of ⅜in (1cm) has been included throughout.

Materials
½yd (.4m) of 36in (90cm)-wide pale pink cotton fabric for body
⅝yd (.5m) of 36in (90cm)-wide floral printed cotton/wool blend
⅝yd (.5m) of 36in (90cm)-wide solid color cotton/wool blend
½yd (.4m) of 44in (112cm)-wide cream cotton fabric
1⅛yd (1m) of ⅜in (1cm)-wide velvet ribbon in both pale pink and green
1⅛yd (1m) of ⅜in (1cm)-wide cream satin ribbon
1⅛yd (1m) of ⅜in (1cm)-wide lace
2¼yd (2m) of 1¼in (3cm)-wide lace
1oz (25g) dark reddish-brown bouclé yarn
1oz (25g) brown mohair-type yarn
12in (30cm) of white seam binding
Small bunch of pink fabric flowers
Stranded embroidery floss in white, black, dusty and dark pink, dark reddish-brown and moss green
Three small pearl buttons
Suitable stuffing, matching threads
Tracing paper, dressmaker's carbon
Small embroidery hoop

1 Trace the pattern pieces for the body, hand and apron on next pages. Using dressmaker's carbon, trace patterns on wrong side of appropriate fabrics. Cut out, leaving extra fabric around heads on one piece. Trace features from page 127.
2 On body piece with untrimmed heads, trace the features for the sad face and the happy face. When tracing, match up with marked features on body pattern.
3 Using three strands of embroidery floss, embroider both the faces, first mounting fabric in hoop. Work the lips, teardrops, pupils and irises in satin stitch. Work edges of cheeks, nostrils, eye lines and lashes in backstitch. Work eyebrows in split stitch. Use French knots for base of nostrils and eye sparkles. Press on the wrong side; trim away excess fabric.

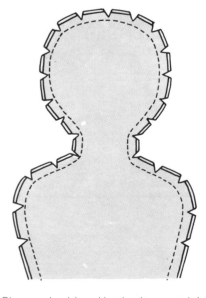

4 Place embroidered body piece on plain body piece with right sides together. Pin, baste and stitch around body, leaving an opening in one side. Clip into seam allowance all around. Turn body right side

out. Stuff body firmly; turn in opening edges and slip stitch them together with tiny stitches.

5 Place hands in pairs with right sides together. Pin, baste and stitch around each pair, leaving wrist edges open. Clip into curves. Turn each hand right side out and stuff it firmly. Pin, baste and stitch across each hand at the wrist.

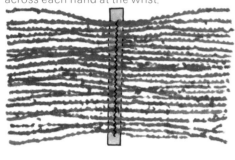

6 To apply hair of sad doll, first cut the seam binding in half. From reddish-brown yarn cut enough pieces 18in (46cm) long to cover binding thickly. Lay the yarn over the binding as shown, leaving $\frac{1}{4}$in (5mm) of binding free at each end. Pin, baste and stitch the yarn to the binding, using a zig-zag stitch. Make the yarn thick enough to cover the head.

7 Place the hair on the head with the sad face so that the zig-zag stitching forms

the center part. Tuck under raw ends of binding to finish them. Backstitch hair to head along center part.

8 Cut cream satin ribbon into four equal pieces. Form a bunch of hair at each side of the head. Tie a length of ribbon around each bunch and into a neat bow. Sew bunches to side of head. Sew a few flowers to each bow.
9 Repeat steps 6 to 8 to make hair for happy face, using pale brown mohair-type yarn.
10 For the petticoat, cut out a piece of cream cotton fabric 32 × 13in (81 × 33cm).
11 Turn under a tiny hem along one long edge of petticoat. Pin, baste and sew in place by hand.

12 Cut a 52in (132cm) length of 1$\frac{1}{4}$in (3cm)-wide lace edging. Run a gathering thread along straight edge of lace edging. Pull up gathering stitches to fit hemmed edge of petticoat. Pin and baste lace to wrong side of petticoat. Pin and baste lace to wrong side of petticoat over hem edge. Stitch in place using a zig-zag stitch.
13 Fold petticoat in half widthwise, wrong sides together and edges matching. Join the side edges with a French seam.

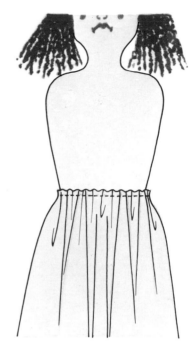

14 Run a gathering thread around top edge of petticoat. Fit the petticoat around the waist edge of doll with wrong side over happy face and seam to center back. Pull up gathering stitches to fit waist and fasten off.
15 Make a tiny double hem around sides of apron. Pin, baste and hand-sew in place.
16 Trace flower motif from apron pattern on page 127. Using dressmaker's carbon paper, trace the motif on right-hand side of apron.
Using three strands of pink and green embroidery floss, work flowers and leaves in chain stitch, backstitch and French knots.
17 For sad doll's skirt cut out one piece of floral-printed fabric 32 × 12in (81 × 30cm).
18 Turn under a tiny double hem along one long edge of skirt. Pin, baste and hem in place by hand.

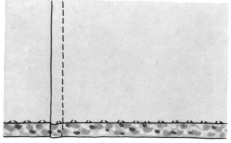

Terry Evans

19 Fold skirt in half widthwise, wrong sides together and edges matching. Pin, baste and stitch the side edges together with a French seam.
20 Run a gathering thread around top edge of skirt. Place skirt over petticoat, right side up, with sad face showing and seam to center back. Draw up gathering stitches to fit waist and fasten off threads securely.

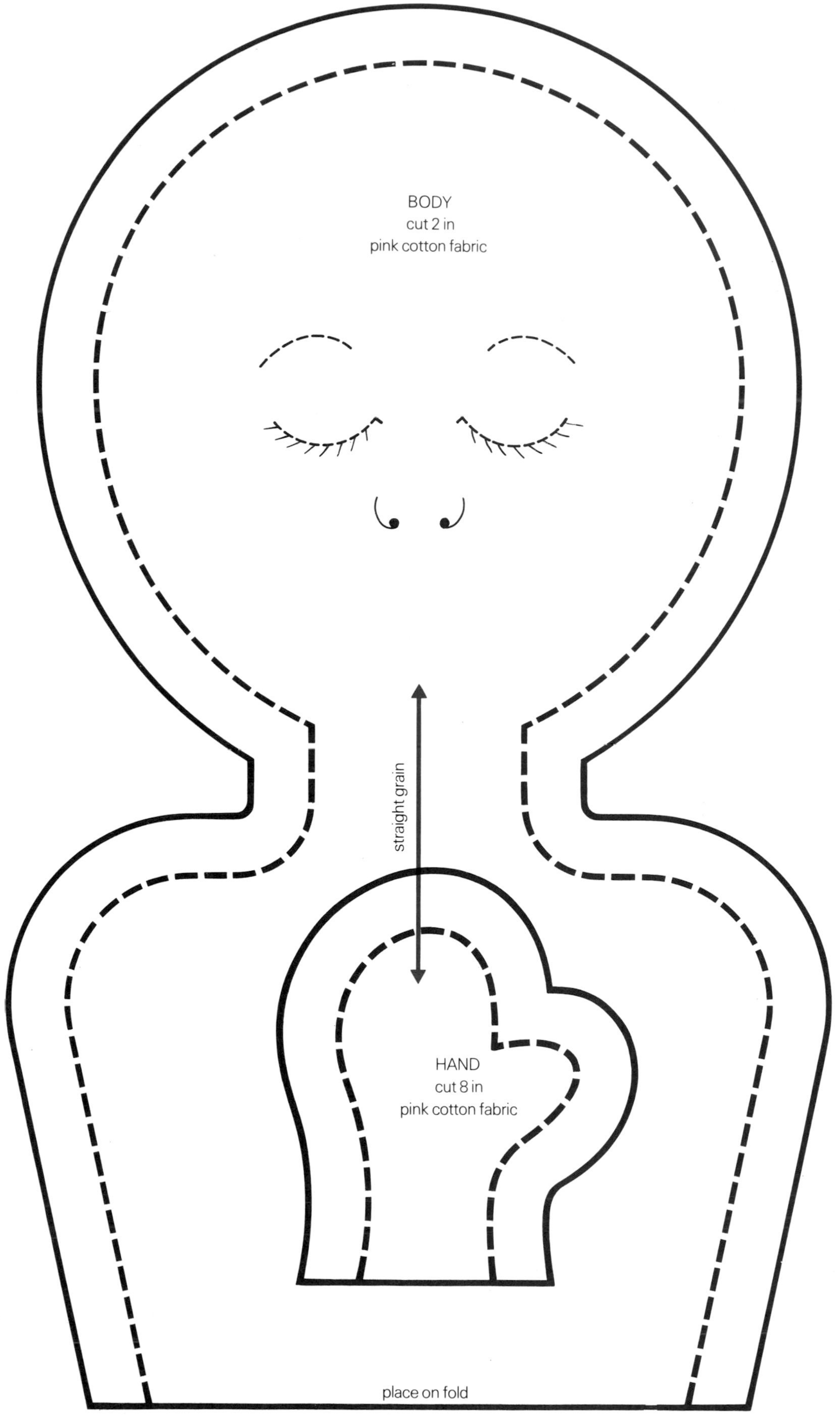
BODY
cut 2 in
pink cotton fabric
straight grain
HAND
cut 8 in
pink cotton fabric
place on fold

Brian Mayor

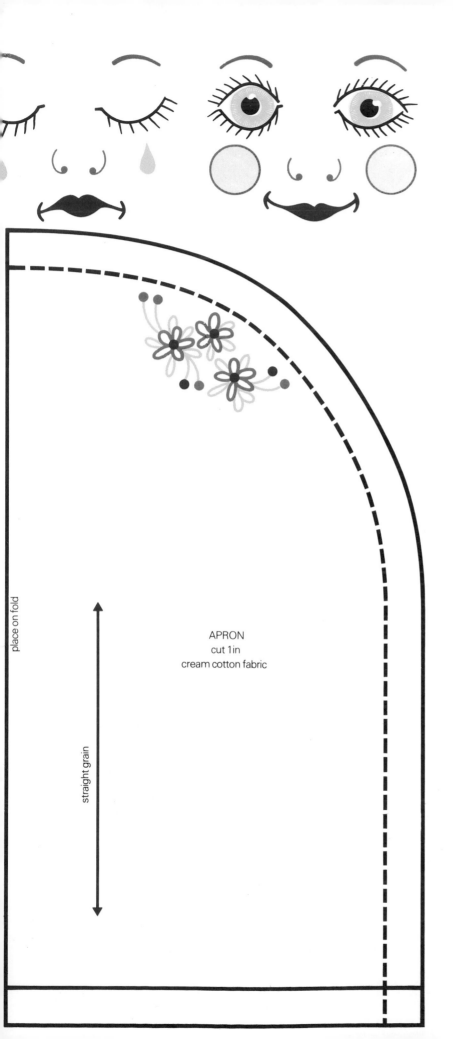

21 Repeat steps 17 to 19 to make a skirt in plain fabric for the happy doll in the same way.

22 Place apron on the center of plain skirt, opposite seam, matching top edges; baste in place. Run a gathering thread around top edge of skirt, including apron. Place skirt/apron over doll, right side up and happy face showing. Draw up gathering to fit waist; fasten off securely.

23 For sad doll's sleeves cut out two pieces from floral-printed fabric, each 6in (15cm) square.

24 Fold sleeves in half, right sides together. Pin, baste and stitch side seams. Turn sleeves right side out.

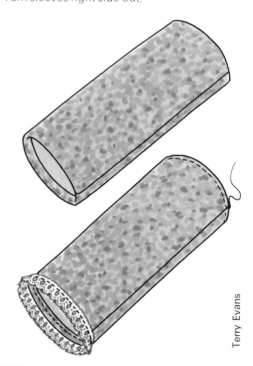

25 Turn under $\frac{3}{8}$in (1cm) at one end of each sleeve. Pin, baste and stitch in place. Cut two 6in (15cm) pieces of narrow lace edging. Placing right sides together, pin, baste and sew each piece of lace edging into a ring. Pin, baste and sew lace edging around hem edge of each sleeve with running stitches; do not fasten off.

APRON
cut 1 in
cream cotton fabric

place on fold

straight grain

Terry Evans

127

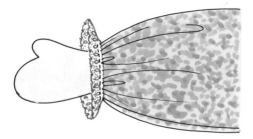

26 Place a hand inside the lace-edged end of each sleeve. Pull up gathering tightly around wrists and fasten off.
27 Repeat steps 23 to 26 using solid-color fabric to make sleeves with hands for happy doll.
28 For sad doll cut a piece of floral-printed fabric measuring 10 × 8in (25 × 20cm) for bodice.

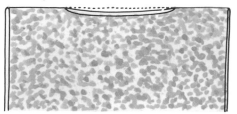

29 Fold bodice in half lengthwise, right sides together and edges matching. Cut a narrow slit along the fold edge for the neck opening, making it large enough to get the head through.

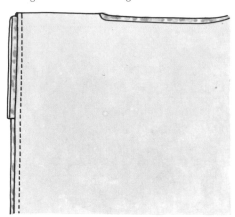

30 Place sleeves inside bodice with tops of sleeves to bodice shoulders. Pin, baste and stitch side seams, catching in sleeves. Trim and turn right side out.

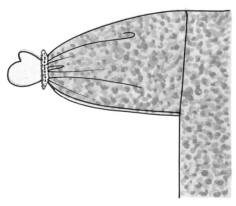

31 Turn under ⅜in (1cm) at lower edge. Pin, baste and sew with running stitches; do not fasten off.

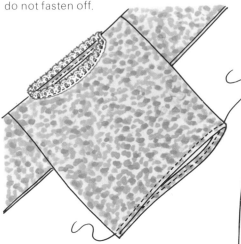

32 Turn under ⅜in (1cm) at neck edge of bodice. Cut a piece of narrow lace edging to fit neck edge plus seam allowance. Placing right sides together, pin, baste and sew edging into a ring. Place lace edging on right side of neck hem. Pin, baste and sew around neck edge with running stitches. Do not fasten off.

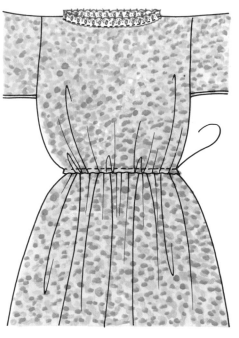

33 Place bodice on sad doll; draw up gathering stitches to fit the doll's waist, covering the raw upper edge of skirt and fasten off the gathering thread securely. Draw up the neckline gathering stitches to fit the doll's neck and fasten off thread securely.
34 Repeat steps 28 to 33 to make the solid-color bodice for the happy doll. Sew three buttons to the center front of the solid-color bodice, spacing them at equal intervals down the front and placing the first button ¾in (2cm) down from the neck edge.

35 Pin, baste and sew the green velvet ribbon around the waist of floral dress and tie in a bow at center front. Slip some flowers into the ribbon at the waist.
36 Pin, baste and sew the pink velvet ribbon around waist of solid-color dress and tie in a bow at center front.
37 Sew a few flowers to the right hand of sad doll.